36 Complete Church DINNER PROGRAMS

Adell Harvey & Mari González

Abingdon Press
NASHVILLE

36 COMPLETE CHURCH DINNER PROGRAMS

Copyright © 1992 by Abingdon Press

Library of Congress Cataloging-in-Publication Data

Harvey, Adell.
    36 complete church dinner programs / Adell Harvey and Mari Gonzalez.
        p. cm.
    Include index.
    ISBN 0-687-41885-2 (alk. paper)
        1. Church dinners. I. Gonzalez, Mari, 1957–   . II. Title.
    III. Title: Thirty-six complete church dinner programs.
    BV1635.H36   1992
    259'.8—dc20   92-7317
                                                                                      CIP

This book is printed on recycled, acid-free paper.

All scripture quotations marked KJV are from the King James Version of the Bible.

All scripture quotations marked NIV are from The New International Version. Copyright © 1978 by The New York International Bible Society. Used by permission.

All scripture quotations marked RSV are from the Revised Standard Version of the Bible, copyrighted 1946, 1952, © 1971, 1973 by the Division of Christian Education of the National Council of the Churches of Christ in the U.S.A. and are used by permission.

MANUFACTURED IN THE UNITED STATES OF AMERICA

In memory of Edith M. Crawford,
whose faith in us turned aspiration into achievement

Acknowledgments

Heartfelt thanks to the many women's groups who have entertained us at their banquets and allowed us to "steal" their ideas. A special thanks to Oak Grove Evangelical Bible Church, Alta Gardens Baptist Church, Alliance Covenant Church, and the Pekin Bible Church, from whom we gleaned numerous party themes. We are also grateful to Rosemary Frantz, who shared her plans for the "Armor of God" banquet.

Contents

CONTENTS

SENSATIONAL OCCASIONS

SIMPLE SUGGESTIONS

INDEXES

Introduction

Have your church potlucks gone to pot, deteriorated to the same old eat-speak-eatcetera rut? Do you frequently wish the covered dishes would stay that way?

As a pastor's wife and home missionary who's been guest at enough potlucks coast to coast to stuff a grizzly, I've seen it all. And I can tell you something: Church potlucks are here to stay! If there's one "paraphrase" of scripture that all denominations agree on, it's this: "Where two or three are gathered together in my name, thou shalt serve a potluck dinner."

Here's the good news! With only a minimum of extra effort, you and your committee can create a potluck that really will keep folks coming back for more (and we don't mean just for food!).

36 Complete Church Dinner Programs is your recipe for hitting the potluck jackpot. Included in these humorous how-to pages are complete menus, themes, decorations, and programs for thirty-six potluck dinners. The ideas are adaptable for every size of congregation, from the grandiose to the very small, from churches that can afford to buy fresh flowers for every table to churches that must grow their own.

Whether you look under the Seasonal, Scriptural, or Sensational headings, you'll find enough ideas and additional idea starters for several years' worth of dinners. We've also given suggestions for adapting the themes to whatever the occasion—or age level—calls for, whether it's a teen buffet, a missionary tea, or a father-son barbecue. You'll also find quick-fix suggestions, punch recipes, quantities for a crowd, and much, much more in this eatery encyclopedia.

So if you're serious about potluck perk up (without potluck prostration), this is the book for you!

Getting Your Potluck Committee Cookin'

The first step in getting a successful potluck, dinner, or food party of any kind cooking is to select an enthusiastic committee. Once you've read a few of the ideas in 36 *Complete Church Dinner Programs*, your own enthusiasm will be so contagious your committee will catch right on.

Then comes the fun. Take a lesson from the Madison Avenue moguls who dream up all those clever and unforgettable TV commercials and turn your committee loose at a brainstorming session. There's only one rule in brainstorming: *Every idea that pops into your mind and out of your mouth is fair game.* Nothing is too absurd to be considered. Some ideas will be wild and wacky; others will be simply wonderful. At the brainstorming stage, write them all down. You can always sort them later!

As you brainstorm, keep in mind *theme, program, decorations,* and *menu.* Remember, stay loose, be original, and let your creativity shine. Who says you can't celebrate Christmas in July or use quilts for table covers? Your theme, for instance, could feature a country, a holiday, a season, an event, a Scripture verse, a cartoon character, an occasion, a book title—the possibilities are endless.

Once the rush of brainstorming ideas is past, go over your list. Discard ideas that are too expensive, too dangerous, or too far out. Cluster the ideas that are left into four groups: theme, program, decorations, and menu. Choose the best ideas that coordinate and presto! You have the outline for an unforgettable church potluck.

Now it's time for another handy-dandy Madison Avenue technique called the *scrounge*. This simply means you raid everything and anything to come up with your party decorations. Look at everything in your house with a new eye and consider: "How can I use this particular item to fit our theme?"

Check out the kids' toy box, your own jewelry box, utensil drawers, knick-knack shelves, gardening sheds, closets, bookshelves, linen closets, and basement or garage stowaway areas. Raid the fishing tackle or tool box and be sure to forage in Grandma's attic or trunk! You may not believe it, but somewhere in all that familiar mess you'll uncover perfect decorations for your party. For instance, you could use the kids' stuffed animals for a "Winnie the Pooh" party. Old bedspreads might see new service as colorful tablecloths. And an old, dilapidated rod and reel might be just the line you need to throw at a father-son fish feast.

Use the scrounge to drum up program content, too. Don't overlook your community resources, such as libraries and resource people. Libraries abound with program ideas, free films, records, and filmstrips. Exchange students, visiting missionaries, people who have traveled extensively, travel bureaus, and chambers of commerce can provide you with colorful first-hand materials for a program that will keep your potluck guests entranced.

Happy scrounging!

And now, the potlucks . . . !

Seasonal
Celebrations

January

WINTER FESTIVAL

January is the perfect month for a snowball retreat, a Saturday sledding party, or other outdoor activities—just the thing for youth or, at least, the young at heart! If you live in a warm climate, use your imagination and bring the snow inside via wintry decorations and pseudo-snow games.

Decorations

Give extended life to some of your Christmas decorations before you stuff them into the attic for another year. Snow-decked gingerbread houses, pine cones, flocked greens, sugar cube igloos, and foam or yarn snowmen look fresh and new when surrounded by white tablecloths and wintry snow scenes, minus the strictly Yuletide elements. Cut huge snowflakes from white paper and hang them from the ceiling and walls to transform your fellowship hall into a Winter Wonderland. Make excellent "skating ponds" from silver foil and ruffle white sheets into snowdrifts.

Menu

There is one rule here: Keep it white! For an outdoor affair, steaming bowls of clam or potato chowder warm the tummy.

Now is the time for a super treat—gigantic mounds of vanilla ice cream, complete with miniature skiers (available at most cake decorating shops). You may want to aim for the world's record for the biggest ice cream sundae.

For a more formal winter scene, try lobster in white sauce or heaping platters of whitefish or turkey breast. Other white offerings include fluffy whipped potatoes, white gravies, cottage cheese, lemon gelatin with cream cheese, marshmallows, and white breads.

Program

An outdoor frolic will furnish all the activity you need, whether it be skiing, skating, or sledding. However, warm climate fortunates will have to make do with other alternatives. Free promotional ski films are available from many resort area chambers of commerce (Jackson Hole, Wyoming; Aspen, Colorado; and Sun Valley, Idaho, to name a few). Some larger libraries and sports shops also have ski or winter sports films.

Youths or juniors would enjoy a make-believe snowball fight, using wads of old newspaper. These same "snowballs" can be used in a variety of games—Snowball 21 with a hula hoop, target tosses, and snowball relays.

Snowball 21 is played like the popular basketball game, using a hula hoop or wastebasket for the basketball hoop and wadded paper "snowballs" as the basketball. The first person to score twenty-one is the winner. In similar fashion, the well-known "horse" basketball game could be played. The first player shoots from any position on the floor, and the player who follows must match the shot. A miss earns the player a penalty point of "H," and each succeeding miss earns another letter of the word *horse*. When a person's misses spell out the entire word, that person is eliminated from the game. The last person out is the winner. A snowball relay can be played with ice cubes, with each team receiving one small cube. Players run relay fashion to a specified line, return the ice cube to the next player on the team, and so on until the ice cube has melted or each team member has run the race.

Devotions

Since this is essentially a party designed for the young at heart, devotions could be in the form of a Bible verse hunt. Use a concordance to locate passages that refer to snow, then divide into teams to see who can find them the quickest.

Scripture idea starters for a speaker's devotional include Job 38:22; Psalm 147:16; Psalm 148:5, 8; Isaiah 55:10-11; Job 9:30 (King James Version); Psalm 51:7; Isaiah 1:18.

Variations

This basic idea could also be used for a missionary emphasis on Alaska, featuring Alaskan snowfish or crab as the main dish and baked Alaska for dessert. Use slides or information on Alaska for the program.

February

ROUGHING IT

There's a lot to celebrate in February, because so many "pioneers" were born that month, including two of the most famous "pioneer" presidents of the United States: George Washington, our first and, therefore, pioneering president, and Abraham Lincoln, whose log-cabin birthplace makes him a pioneer. Babe Ruth, Charles Lindbergh, Thomas Edison, Henry Wadsworth Longfellow, and Charles Dickens may not have broken sod, split logs, or worn coonskin hats, but they were pioneers in their fields.

February is also Black History Month, a special time to honor all those brave men and women who pioneered the entry of blacks into new areas of endeavor. To wrap all the events of the month together, stage a pioneer day, encouraging everyone to dress as a pioneer in any field.

Decorations

Deck the tables in quilts, with miniature log cabins as centerpieces, or heap a pile of twigs, craftsticks, or Lincoln logs in the middle of each table. Before the meal begins, have the guests at each table compete to see who can build the quickest, biggest, most original, or best log cabin. The winning table is served first.

Axes, antique tools, ox yokes, crocks, or jars of home-canned foods and jellies can be added for more atmosphere.

Menu

Each family brings a prepared meal to be auctioned off in the tradition of the old-fashioned box social. Breaking with tradition, other families bid on the boxes and eat whichever meal they purchase. The money raised from the auction could go to a missionary pioneering in a new field or to a relief agency pioneering in aid to Third World countries or to inner-city missions in our own country.

Or try a soul-food special, complete with black-eyed peas, grits, and corn bread.

Provide dessert in the form of cherry cheesecake, cherry pie, or log cupcakes. Make the log cupcakes by putting two cupcakes end to end and covering completely with chocolate frosting, grooved to resemble bark. Decorate with a paper axe and a sprig of cherries.

Program

If your church uses wood as a heat source or for a fireplace in the fellowship hall, your chopped wood supply is probably getting low by now. Have a log-splitting contest. It will be fun and will result in a renewed stock of cut firewood.

Since February is the month of Longfellow's birth, you could read some of his poetry. Or you could read Lincoln's Gettysburg Address. Resident poets in your group may want to share some of their original poems. Or you could play charades or have a fun quiz using events from the lives of the famous people born in this month.

Devotions

Scripture readings should center around the pioneers in the Bible, such as Abraham and Sarah, or other greats who have left their footprints in the sands of time. If you are using the proceeds from the box social for a missionary offering, you could incorporate the work of that missionary into the devotions.

Other Events to Celebrate in February

- In honor of the world-famous groundhog, try a "Pig Out" party around February 2.

- An "Invention Convention" would be a fun way to celebrate Thomas Edison's birthday (February 11, 1847).

- The Feast of Purim, which celebrates the Jews' triumph over evil and oppression, usually falls in February. Traditional celebrations include Thanksgiving-like feasts, costume balls, and carnivals.

March

SPUD PARTY

In honor of that great honorary Irishman, St. Patrick, the Irish potato will move from its usual place as a side dish and take center stage tonight.

Decorations

The spud will be star, so anything to do with potatoes can set the decor. Centerpieces can be large potatoes, decorated to look like people. Use your imagination and turn ordinary potatoes into Cowboy Spud, Spec Tater, Ro Tater, Hesi Tater, Imi Tater, and Agi Tater. Thumbtacks make easy eyes; yarn or wisps of cotton fluff up for hair, mustaches, and beards; slivers of red pimiento, construction paper, or felt can be shaped into mouths. Craft sticks protruding from the bottom of the spuds serve as legs and also support the potatoes, or you can flatten the bottom of the potato to make it sit erect. Finish your creations with scraps of cloth for neckties, skirts, or hats.

If decorating potatoes exceeds your creativity, simply arrange mounds of potatoes in baskets or on scraps of burlap for centerpieces, sticking in straw flowers here and there for a bit of color.

Your grocer may give you colorful potato promotional

posters to hang about the room. You can also write for them from the Idaho Potato Commission, P.O. Box 1068, Boise, Idaho 83701. Also available from the Potato Commission, usually free for the asking, are marvelous potato recipes and spud lapel pins to give away as party favors.

Menu

Potatoes, what else? There are as many ways to serve potatoes as there are eyes on the earthy tuber. A simple menu could feature potato chowder served with crackers and dessert.

How about potato pancakes and sausage? For a less organized bash, just make the announcement, "Everyone bring a favorite potato dish." You'll be amazed at the varieties they'll come up with, bless their potato-cooking little hearts!

You might serve the meal cafeteria style, with heaps of plain baked potatoes at the head of the table. Along the route, guests have their choice of numerous toppings to adorn their spud—chili, broccoli and cheese sauce, beef stroganoff, creamed chipped beef. Check out restaurant potato bars for more ideas. Bacon bits, shredded cheese, sour cream, butter, sprouts, sunflower seeds, and various other garnishes can be set out, salad bar fashion.

For a light luncheon, you may feature ham rolls stuffed with potato salad and served with a variety of potato chips. For a unique dessert, serve ice cream made from potato flakes. A new product, it may be hard to find in some areas. But it's worth the hunt as it only has ninety calories per serving.

Program

Naturally, the master of ceremonies will be a Common Tater. You could feature a skit, using Imi, Agi, Ro, and Spec

Tater in an old-fashioned melodrama. And don't forget to throw in a part for everyone's heroine, Sweet Tater.

If someone in your group is a dimestore-variety magician, why not feature him or her as the Amazing Prestidigi Tater?

Music should feature good old Irish songs, perhaps a sing-along reminiscent of old Killarney.

If children are present, they would enjoy reenacting the legend of St. Patrick's march across the Emerald Isle to rid the country of its snakes. Many libraries also have filmstrip stories of this event.

Devotions

Again, the Tater family—Ro, his wife, Agi, and their children, Spec, Hesi, and Imi—could be used as object lessons. Or you might use the Genesis account of the serpent's beguiling Eve. The Revelation 12:9 reference to "that old serpent" could be used to explain the snake imagery of the St. Patrick story.

April

RAINBOWS OF PROMISE

Everyone knows that "April showers bring May flowers"—with those showers come rainbows. What better way to celebrate spring than with rainbows to remind your guests of God's promises?

Decorations

Use rainbow bedecked sheets or a rainbow painted brightly on newsprint as a wall banner. If you use a sheet, pin the theme to it; otherwise, print the theme on the newsprint. Hang rainbows and colorful umbrellas about the room. Use small umbrellas planted beside bright flowers for centerpieces, or use rainbow-colored dolls and accessories to deck the table.

For tablecloths, use pastel sheets in the colors of the rainbow or newsprint with rainbows drawn on. Pastel paper plates, napkins, and utensils with rainbow motifs or stickers will add to the decor.

At each place setting, plant a flower in edible "dirt." Use cups that resemble flower pots; paper cups will work. Pack the cups with vanilla ice cream. Cover the ice cream with crumbled dark chocolate cookies to resemble dirt, and plant an artificial flower in each cup. Keep the "flower pots" in the freezer until banquet time so that the ice cream will remain hard.

Menu

Serve ham, mixed vegetables, layered gelatins, and green salads for a colorful spring feast. Rainbow sherbet is an alternate dessert choice. For a fun touch, put rainbow-colored cereal in bowls along the tables for extra nibbles.

Program

Stage a treasure hunt with everyone looking for the pot of gold at the end of the rainbow. Your "pot" could be full of more colorful cereal, golden candy corn, or gold foil-wrapped mints.

Have a fun quiz about rainbows: How many colors are in the rainbow? Name the colors of the rainbow. Or discuss some of the curious scientific facts about this colorful phenomenon. Encourage people to bring and display rainbow photos; just about anyone who owns a camera has at least one rainbow shot. Make creative rain gear from plastic garbage bags for a novel fashion show, or use the idea for a table vs. table contest.

Sing songs, either secular or spiritual, about rainbows and rain. Songs like "Somewhere Over the Rainbow," "Joy Is Like the Rain," or "Showers of Blessing" fit in nicely.

Devotions

A short talk on God's many promises, a Bible verse hunt to locate scriptural promises, or the story of Noah would wrap the meal up on a thoughtful note.

May

IN HONOR OF VETERANS

While the government has done much to set aside days to remember the veterans who have given their lives and their youth to serve the country, and the media extend themselves to recall anniversaries of battles, both recent and dated, churches seldom follow suit. Yet the veterans of the church may have much to share about the suffering they have seen as well as about God's provision in times of trial. A program honoring the church's veterans would fit in at any patriotic holiday, particularly Memorial Day, Veterans Day, or Armed Forces Day.

Decorations

Red, white, and blue naturally will be your color scheme. Ask the veterans to bring souvenirs from the countries they served in, their medals, old uniforms, and photo albums. Use these for centerpieces and decorations. Try to get framed photos of the vets in their uniforms for display.

Menu

Serve food from the countries in which your veterans served, or have C-rations—the infamous "SOS" (creamed chipped beef over toast), dehydrated potatoes, black coffee, beef jerky, scrambled eggs, canned fruit cocktail, carrot and raisin salad—the not-so-favorite foods every veteran remembers.

Program

A fashion show of the old uniforms will bring many laughs. Allow time for guests to browse through photo albums and to ask the veterans questions. This provides a good opportunity for the veterans to share their testimonies or war anecdotes, and it is a time to pray for the young people of the church who are serving in the armed forces. In this day and age, they can use all the prayer they can get.

You could also put together "care packages" for those in the armed forces. The vets can fill you in on the best way you can minister to those currently in the military. Provide note paper or humorous cards and invite guests to write a note of encouragement to those who are serving their country.

For a more informal program, schedule your dinner around the annual Army-Navy football game and invite all the veterans to come watch the game together. Get good-natured rivalry going between the Army veterans and the "ducks."

Devotions

The Bible abounds with histories of battles and great warriors who depended on God. Do a short study on the warfare in the Bible or tell the story of a biblical warrior, such as David, Deborah, Gideon, or Joshua.

June

BLAZING THE TRAIL

Since fathers and mothers are special, this event honors them. It can be adapted for a banquet or for a special breakfast-in-the-park outing for the whole family.

Decorations

Parents blaze the trail for their youngsters to follow, and because children usually want to walk in their parents' footsteps, a western cowboy motif suits the trailblazers. Lasso your way to easy decorations. Other rope tricks include lariats and maybe some fancy knotwork. Display saddles, cowboy hats and boots, and model horses; cut ranch brands from construction paper or burn them into wooden slabs.

Menu

A hefty beef barbecue suitable for rugged ranch hands is perfect for the roundup. If this is a carry-in dinner, families can bring their favorite dishes.

For a breakfast event, sausage, hashbrowns, eggs, and pancakes are scrumptious when grilled over an open fire. Serve with hot chocolate and plenty of strong, black coffee.

Program

A cowboy campfire sing-along is fun, with everyone yodeling along on songs like "Home on the Range," "Get Along Little Dogie," "Back in the Saddle Again," and "Tumblin' Tumbleweeds."

New words set to familiar music make good sing-alongs, too. For example, you might sing "Onward, Christian Parents" (set to the tune of "Onward, Christian Soldiers").

> Onward, Christian parents,
> Lead us on our way.
> We pray God will bless you
> On this special day.
> With your lives to teach us,
> We will ever be
> Walking on the pathway
> To life eternally.
>
> (Chorus)
> Onward, Christian parents,
> Lighting up our way.
> God bless Christian parents
> Today and every day.

Or you might try "We've a Song to Sing About Parents" (set to the tune of "We've a Story to Tell to the Nations").

> We've a song to sing about parents;
> To thank them for all that they do.
> A song of times, past and present,
> Of the time they've spent with you.
> Oh, parents, we do love you.
>
> (Chorus)
> For our parents are at the ready,
> Whether at work or at play.
> They help at church and again at school;
> Bless parents, Lord, each day.

29

> We've a song to sing about parents,
> A song of their love and care,
> For they have worked many hours,
> To provide for all our needs.
> Our parents love you and me.

Hobby-horse races are hilarious, and the kids would get a charge out of seeing their folks racing on stick horses. A horsey-back relay race, with the parents down on all fours and their offspring astraddle, could also be a winner.

If you can invite someone who does rope tricks or can do a roping demonstration, the children (young and old) would love you forever!

Devotions

Scripture contains much good advice for parents. Deuteronomy 6:4-6 or Ephesians 6:4 are good starting points.

Other Events to Celebrate in June

- June is a great month for staging a church homecoming or reunion with an old-fashioned dinner on the grounds.

- Fly the flag in honor of Flag Day and get a head start on patriotic celebrations.

- Sponsor an all-night graduation fling for your local high school seniors.

July

SEE THE U.S.A.

A patriotic theme sparkles for the Fourth of July application, but it lends itself just as well to a number of different seasons: in February in honor of Presidents' Day, in May for Memorial Day, in June for Flag Day, in September for Labor Day, or in November for Veterans Day. Use the theme at any time to honor a returning member of the service or at a farewell party for military families. During election years, a patriotic theme serves as a fun election night bash or in place of an inaugural ball.

Decorations

Fly the colors! Red, white, and blue bunting, streamers, flowers, candles, stars, flags—decorations are limited only by your budget and space.

A large paper scroll printed in Old English script with "We the people . . ." makes an excellent constitutional backdrop. Similar scrolls in miniature can serve as centerpieces, accompanied by turkey-feather quills inserted in tiny bottles. Small American flags, bought in packets from the local stationery store, can be stuck in red gumdrops as party favors. Red, white, and blue crêpe paper streamers twisted down the center of a white table cover accent the brave, bold mood. Miniature

Statues of Liberty, Liberty Bells, or other patriotic memorabilia also make excellent and easy centerpieces.

Show off America "from sea to shining sea." For a slightly different twist, borrow souvenirs from the congregation's travels across the United States for display. Driftwood from the Pacific coastal areas; seashells from the Atlantic; cactus from the Southwest; wood products from the north woods—your friends' collections will surprise and delight you. Large travel maps will also help you recreate "America the Beautiful."

Menu

What's more American than hamburgers, hot dogs, fried chicken, potato salad, apple pie, and watermelon?

For a more detailed menu, pick up on an individual state's theme. Assign people to bring foods from various regions: gumbo or creole from Louisiana; okra, grits, and corn bread from the South; Spanish-style delicacies and Navajo fry bread from the Southwest; corn on the cob from the Midwest; fish dishes from the coastal areas; potatoes from Idaho or Maine.

Program

Begin the program with the Pledge of Allegiance and "The Star Spangled Banner."

Assign someone to present a slide show, featuring a few slides from each family's vacation assortment as well as patriotic slides, which can be bought from gift shops at most major airports. Patriotic music provides a stirring backdrop for slides of America's historical monuments.

A sing-along is a must for this party; Americans don't get enough opportunities to sing the great inspiring songs of the nation!

Invite a local history professor, a member of the Daughters of the American Revolution, or an avid history buff to give a brief historical sketch of a national monument near your area.

You may wish to adapt the following program to your particular situation. (Many of the ideas are adapted from *America, God Shed His Grace on Thee,* published by Moody Press, 1975.) Our family singing group, the "Harvey-Farley Happy Sounds," used it successfully in numerous churches throughout the country.

Fantastic, Funtastic America

Narrator: No one will ever fully understand why it has pleased God to bless the United States of America with an abundance so rare in history and with freedoms that are an example for the world. Our privileges should make us stop and think. Is this freedom and abundance ours only by chance? Is it wholly due to what we like to think of as American ingenuity? Or are there other, more spiritual factors involved? If God has, indeed, blessed America, why? Could we be in danger of suddenly losing the blessings we have for so long enjoyed?

One of our most moving patriotic hymns reminds us of the beauty of America. As Katherine Lee Bates stood atop Pike's Peak and scanned the sweep of the land, she wrote of "purple mountain majesties and amber waves of grain" and concluded that God had shed his grace on this land. With proper respect for the other nations and tribes of earth, Americans can still sing in good conscience: "America! America! God shed his grace on thee."

All: "America, the Beautiful"

Narrator: The purple mountain majesties and the fruited plains indeed originated with God. America's blessings surpass those of many nations of the earth and should inspire thanksgiving in all who enjoy them. The great spiritual foundation

33

that built America has unfolded by remarkable design. So also did American democracy, along with our Constitution and the great freedom it ensures.

No, the development of America did not happen by chance, as is obvious to any person who understands the events that shaped this nation.

Tonight we want to highlight some of the things that helped make our land great, not for the purpose of looking back, but that we should better understand where America is today, how we arrived here, and where we must turn at this critical hour in our history. Let's all stand and thank God for America!

Prayer

Slide Narrator: Many of our church families have had the chance to see much of this great land of ours and have loaned their vacation slides for us to enjoy. So, settle back and take an armchair excursion with us across this great and beloved country of ours. As we travel, think about God's goodness to America, about our freedoms, and about our tremendous spiritual heritage. And sing along with us as we go!

Patriotic Medley: Recordings of "This Is My Country," "Battle Hymn of the Republic," "America," and any other familiar patriotic songs to accompany slides. Suit the slides to the following narration. (Note: Projecting slides of the Statue of Liberty, of the Lincoln Memorial, of a penny, of purple mountains, of amber waves of grain, and so on at the appropriate places greatly enhances this program. If slides are not available, an opaque projector can be rented from most camera centers; these can project any photo or painting onto a screen or other surface. Calendars are a great source of pictures for such projection, as are *Ideals* publications.)

Reader 1: A beautiful place, our America! America was made great, not by its beautiful fields, but by those who work the fields; not by its factories, but by the laborers who run the machinery; not by its towering forests, but by the families who have used their products and reforested their acres. The people have made America a great nation!

Reader 2: People! America's greatest resource, its greatest asset. They pioneered a continent, subdued the elements, molded a society of folk from all over the world. Like no other nation, America became a melting pot for the peoples of the world, blending cultures, traditions, and languages into one great American dream. Even today millions still seek freedom within our shores—those who have known persecution in other lands know best what the United States and its liberties truly mean.

One of those freedom-seeking immigrants, Rabbi Abba Hillel Silver, saw the hand of God on America when he wrote:

Male Reader: (wearing Hebrew yarmulke and prayer shawl)

God built him a continent of glory, and filled it with treasures untold. He studded it with sweet-flowering fountains, and traced it with long-winding streams. He carpeted it with soft-rolling prairies, and columned it with thundering mountains. He graced it with deep-shadowed forests, and filled them with song.

Then he called unto a thousand peoples, and summoned the bravest among them. They came from the ends of the earth, each bearing a gift and a hope. The glow of adventure was in their eyes, and in their hearts the glory of hope.

And out of the bounty of earth, and the labor of men; out of the longing of heart, and the prayer of souls; out of the memory of ages, and the hopes of the world, God fashioned a nation in love, and blessed it with purpose sublime.

And they called it America!

Narrator: Like no other nation, America has opened its arms and heart to God's chosen people. New York City alone is home to more Jews than live in the entire nation of Israel. They've added their own unique stamp to America's culture, with bagels and blintzes, lox and leffels. Let's try singing some of their music!

All: Try a few choruses of Hebrew music. (The "Hava N'gila" is familiar to most people, as is "Shalom Chaverim," which can be found in the Girl Scout songbook *Sing Together*.)

Narrator: Likewise, people of Spanish descent have added their particular charm to our heritage.

Children: Sing the chorus of "Jesus Loves Me" in Spanish.

>Cristo me ama,
>Cristo me ama,
>Cristo me ama,
>La Biblia dice a si.

(These Spanish words are phonetically pronounced: *"Krees'-toh may ah'-mah . . . lah Bee'-blee-ah dee'-say ah-see'."*)

Reader: One of the first sights to greet newcomers to our shores is the giant copper statue on Liberty Island in New York Harbor, the awesome lady whose official name is "Liberty Enlightening the World."

Solo: "The Cross Is My Statue of Liberty"

Reader: Another great symbol of our liberty is that beautiful star-spangled banner, the flag that unites us all as "one nation under God."

Since the first American flag, bearing thirteen stripes and thirteen stars and the crosses of St. George and St. Andrew, was first flown over Cambridge, Massachusetts, on January 2,

1776, our flag has undergone many changes. On June 14, 1777, the Second Continental Congress resolved to formally adopt the stars and stripes as the official flag of the United States of America.

In 1818 Congress decreed that a new star should be added each time a new state joined the Union. On January 3, 1960, the fiftieth star, representing the state of Hawaii, was added to the flag, giving us the fifty-star banner we proudly salute tonight.

Narrator: As the American flag symbolizes our nation, the Christian banner reminds us of our dual citizenship, our double heritage. Let's stand and salute the Christian flag, following with one verse of "Onward, Christian Soldiers."

All: (Christian Flag Salute) "I pledge allegiance to the Christian flag, and to the Savior for whose kingdom it stands. One Savior, crucified, risen, and coming again, with life and liberty to all who believe."

Narrator: One factor contributing to America's greatness is leaders who depend on God, leaders who pray before making major decisions.

Reader 3: The Lincoln Memorial in Washington, D.C., pays fitting homage to one of our greatest presidents, Abraham Lincoln. No other president so deeply believed and so consistently demonstrated that Almighty God rules in the affairs of earth.

Born in obscurity in a humble log cabin, Lincoln learned to study and memorize the Scriptures at his mother's knee. Even as a boy, he seemed to understand that God directs history. Lincoln knew his Bible well and could quote it with ease. The biblical phrase "a house divided against itself cannot stand" became his plea for the preservation of the Union.

During trying times in New Salem, Illinois, Lincoln struggled with his faith, causing some to brand him an infidel. But, unmistakably, his spiritual convictions deepened as he assumed the role of president and faced the problems of slavery and the Civil War.

Lincoln arose every day at 4:00 A.M. to read his Bible and pray before beginning a busy day at the White House. Many people have told of hearing him cry out in agonizing prayer to God during times of added stress.

Thank God for leaders, like Abraham Lincoln, who knew how to pray!

All: "God of Our Fathers"

Reader 4: Suppose our civilization were destroyed and our cities laid waste. Suppose that in twenty thousand years an archaeologist from another society poked around the ruins of our city. If that person could dig up but one small penny, a great deal would be told about us.

The coin is made of a blend of metals—that would state that we were miners and knew the science of metallurgy. By the shape of the coin, a perfect circle, the archaeologist would know we understood geometry. The grain pictured on the back of the older coins would show that we had been a great agricultural society, who considered our crops a major source of our wealth. The date on the face of the coin would show that we understood arithmetic and had a calendar. The portrait of Abraham Lincoln would mark us as artists who had an advanced culture, people who respected and honored our leaders.

The words *United States* would let the archaeologist know that we were a federated group of local communities bound together by a strong central government. The phrase *e pluribus unum* would point out that we were scholars who knew other languages. The word *liberty* inscribed on the face of the penny would let the archaeologist know that our country sought to guarantee freedom for everyone.

And finally, the phrase "In God we trust" would tell the archaeologist that we had a high moral law. It would show that we had grown strong and mighty under God's great hand. Then, considering the penny, the archaeologist might wonder, "Why did they ever go astray?"

Narrator: No, America is not perfect. Our country has scandals, unemployment, inflation, food and fuel shortages, and poverty. There is even a crack in our Liberty Bell!

The Scriptures teach us that God will judge both nations and individuals. But he is also a God of grace. God extends his grace to all those who will come to him, and he offers free salvation to all who will accept his Son, the Lord Jesus Christ. How is your relationship with God tonight? Have you accepted his grace?

Solo: "If That Isn't Love"

Narrator: God often withholds judgment on nations when people turn to him. Second Chronicles 7:14 says, "If my people who are called by my name humble themselves, and pray and seek my face, and turn from their wicked ways, then will I hear from heaven, and will forgive their sin and heal their land" (RSV).

Several times in the history of our nation, a widespread return to God has put people back on course. Each time it has reversed a downward moral trend in society and ultimately has unleashed profound social changes.

Let's pray for America. Our president, congressional delegates, and officials in positions of leadership on the federal, state, and local levels need our intercession. The Bible tells us to remember "all that are in authority; that we may lead a quiet and peaceable life in all godliness and honesty" (I Tim. 2:2 KJV).

Let's all bow for a few moments of silent prayer for our country, then close by singing that heart cry of believers all across this great land, "God Bless America"! As we pray, remember that "only as America blesses God can God bless America!" Shall we pray.

Prayer

All: "God Bless America"

Devotions

If the above program is used, no other devotional time is needed. If the program is not used, Romans 13 and Second Chronicles 7:14 are good launching points for a brief message.

Other Events to Celebrate in July

• Celebrate Christmas in July with a Santa's workshop to get an early start on repairing toys for your local Toys for Tots program.

• Hot summer days are also great for a community Dutch-oven chicken fry, hoedown, or barbecue.

August

HAWAIIAN HOLIDAY

When the heat and humidity of summer become oppressive, nothing sounds quite so refreshing as escape to an exotic, breezy island. Since not everyone can make that escape, create your own island paradise by serving a light salad supper alongside a pool or lake, or bring the mood indoors by transforming your fellowship hall into a South Sea Island retreat. This is a great way to celebrate a very special birthday dinner, an end-of-summer retreat for the youth before they scatter to the four winds, or a mothers' day at the beach.

Decorations

Blue table covers represent sparkling tropical water; beige ones, the island sand. Hawaiian leis, colorful beads, seashells, hunks of coral, or island mementos serve as graceful center-pieces. If the dinner is indoors, a large mirror laid flat and surrounded by flowers, shrubs, rocks, and sand will add a lake-like atmosphere. Wrap basement pillars in brown crêpe paper and wire large green-paper palm branches to the tops to create your own tropical forest. Hawaiian travel posters and background music will further enhance the lush feeling of paradise. A super-ambitious committee can drape black or navy

41

blue gauze from the ceiling, dot it with large foil stars and a few puffs of cloud-like cotton, and add a silver moon for a really enchanted evening.

Have greeters place leis on the guests as they arrive to welcome them in true Hawaiian style. Guests should come dressed in their brightest flowered shirts and dresses, with muumuus a comfortable plus. A prize could be offered for the loudest shirt. Authentic or fake grass skirts will add still more to the fun.

Menu

Light eating is a must when spending an evening at the beach. This is the place to whip up your most creative salads; for a carry-in, ask guests to bring their favorites. Salads come in all sizes and flavors—meat salads, green salads, dessert salads, vegetable salads—you'll be amazed at the variety.

For an elegant look, serve fruit salads in carved watermelon shells and pineapple boats. Accompany your festive fruits with assorted crackers and cheeses arranged in large conch shells. Seashells surrounding a frothy punch bowl complete the look. For a hot meal, try "Shipwreck Casserole" or "Sea-licious Tuna."

Shipwreck Casserole

Layer sliced raw potatoes, chopped celery, grated carrots, and sliced onion in a large baking dish. Cover with a layer of browned lean ground beef, the contents of a large can of kidney beans, and two 1 lb. cans of stewed tomatoes (or tomato soup). Sprinkle with salt and pepper to taste, and bake for two hours at 350 degrees.

Sea-licious Tuna

Place 1½ cups of prepared poultry stuffing in a large greased casserole dish. Top with two 6½ oz. cans of tuna (separated with fork). Blend one can celery soup with the juice and grated rind of ½ lemon and pour over tuna. Sprinkle with grated Parmesan cheese. Bake at 350 degrees for 25 minutes.

Program

If this supper is served poolside, no program is necessary, as the water antics will keep everyone busy. Dog-paddle and crab-leg relays, cork or ping-pong ball harvest, watermelon scramble, and a rousing game of beachball keepaway are good if you want organized activities. For a cork or ping-pong ball harvest, simply throw a bucketful of corks or balls into the pool. When a signal is given, all swimmers dive into the pool and try to retrieve as many balls as possible. The team or individual harvesting the most balls or corks in a given time is the winner. A watermelon placed in the pool makes a slippery, difficult-to-hold-on-to object for a team scramble. The winning team is the group that successfully gets it to the surface and onto the deck. A crab-leg relay is similar to the three-legged races run on land. Two swimmers lock their inside legs and swim the length of the pool, three-legged.

Using this theme in a fellowship hall calls for a bit more ingenuity. Younger people would enjoy "Shipwreck," a variation of "Upset the Fruit Basket." Players are seated in a circle, and each player is given the name of a fish, such as whale, trout, shark, or goldfish. Be sure to repeat fish names so there are several players who have each name. When a fish is called, everyone having that name trades seats. If the leader calls "Shipwreck!" everyone must rush to exchange chairs, the leader included. The person left without a chair is the new leader.

A water balloon toss would make a real splash. You'll need several water balloons in a basket and several bath towels. Divide into couples, giving each couple a towel. One person stands at either end of the towel, holding it taut. A water

43

balloon is placed in the middle of the towel. Each couple uses their towel to toss the balloon to another couple, who then tries to catch it in their towel. When a balloon breaks, replace it with another one.

If the party is held in a park or other outdoor location, wet banana slides or other sprinkler games and water balloons will help your guests forget that they don't have a real pool.

Devotions

Scripture abounds with sea stories. The prophet, Jonah, is a good example of "A Man Overboard!" Jesus' walking on the water in Matthew 14:22-32, stilling the waves in Matthew 8:23-27, or preparing breakfast for the fishermen disciples in John 21 are other suggested topics. The parable of the dragnet in Matthew 13:47 would also fit here.

Other Events to Celebrate in August

- A phenomenon of recent years is neighborhood watch. August is a great month to celebrate "Neighborhood Watch Night Out" so that neighbors can get better acquainted.

- Host an evening gala: "Midsummer Night's Dream"!

September

TRACING YOUR ROOTS

Knowing where you came from can mean a lot to your self-esteem. In today's mobile society, people often forget their family roots, intensifying an unsettled feeling. Have a "Roots Day" to celebrate the family and to give people an opportunity to dig up their family trees.

Decorations

Persuade the resident artist in your group to draw or trace a family tree, such as those found in baby books and family Bibles. Leave the blanks to be filled in later. Make copies of the family tree and use them as placemats. For centerpieces and other decor, ask people to bring their coats of arms, clan tartans, family Bibles, heirlooms, and old family pictures. Quilts used as table covers or lace tablecloths help create a nostalgic atmosphere.

Menu

Everyone should bring a food reminiscent of his or her national heritage. People of mixed nationalities could bring a dish from their most predominant ethnic group. Assign a main course, a dessert, a salad, and bread or a side dish and encourage folks to get out the old family cookbooks to complete their assignment. Your multinational feast could end up including German *sauerbraten*, Middle Eastern *tabuli*, Mexican *flan*, and many other exciting ethnic dishes.

Program

Have families fill out their family trees as much as they can from memory. Collect trees, shuffle, and pass them out again. Each person tries to guess to whom each family tree belongs.

Give the in-house photographer a workout. Have each family don ethnic costumes or antique fashions for an instant family photograph in the vein of the old tintypes.

Since this is a family affair, allow plenty of free time for families to reminisce and fellowship together.

Devotions

Draw up the family tree of Jesus Christ, using Matthew 1 and Luke 3:23-38. Do a study of the four women who appear in Matthew's genealogy, or you could use Exodus 20:12 as a devotional topic. Your song choice might be "Faith of Our Fathers."

Other Events to Celebrate in September

- Try a "School Daze" theme, complete with spelling bees, count downs, lunch boxes, blackboards, and apples for the teacher.
- Honor football players or teams with an athletic banquet.
- Celebrate ancient holidays in new ways, with a Rosh Hashana or a Yom Kippur theme.
- Honor labor unions or the laborers in your group at a Labor Day picnic.

October

INDIAN SUMMER

It's always hard to say good-bye to summer, especially if you live in a climate marked by long, hard winters. Make those beautiful autumn days in October stretch as long as they'll go with a fun-filled Indian Summer celebration.

Decorations

Use fall colors of burnt orange, squash yellow, and nut brown for tablecloths and accessories, with miniature tepees formed from construction paper serving as centerpieces. Or heap the tables with bright autumn leaves, Indian corn, gourds, squash, or other harvest arrangements of fruits and vegetables. Displays of pottery, jewelry, and other artifacts would also enhance this theme.

Menu

Serve some wild-game meat or fish with squash, corn, and pumpkin dishes, Navajo fry bread, and pumpkin pie. Small dishes of candy corn on the tables will add a sweet touch.

Program

Show a filmstrip, such as Walt Disney's "Light in the Forest" (available at most public libraries). It tells the poignant story of a boy who is kidnapped and raised by the Native Americans, and it has a tremendous message of unity.

Read Longfellow's "A Song of Hiawatha" or feature a presentation on ministry in reservations.

Devotions

Discuss the kinship of humanity, tracing humanity's roots from Noah's three sons in Genesis 10. The unity of the church, discussed in Ephesians 4:4-6, also makes a fitting theme.

Other Events to Celebrate in October

Why not try a "Harvest Moon Midnight Supper," or how about celebrating Canadian Thanksgiving Day or the Jewish Feast of Tabernacles (Booths or Succoth)?

November

THY WORD IS A LAMP UNTO MY FEET

The first Sunday in November is International Bible Sunday. National Bible Week also falls in November (the dates vary from year to year). This dinner focuses on that book of all books, the Holy Bible. It can also be used as a vacation Bible school kick-off dinner, a Christian school awards banquet, an installation dinner for Sunday school teachers and officers, or for a Sunday school convention banquet.

Decorations

Light your "lamp" theme with old lanterns, hurricane lamps, or even modern flashlights for centerpieces. Send for free placemats, bookmarks, booklets, Scripture segments, and tracts from sources such as the following:

- American Bible Society, Box 5656, Grand Central Station, New York, NY 10163
- Bible Pathways, Box 1515, Murfreesboro, TN 37133
- Wycliffe Bible Translators, Huntington Beach, CA 92647

Glue half-sheets of paper to craft sticks, then roll up scroll style and tie with ribbon to make individual Scripture scroll favors. Print Bible verses, such as Psalm 119:105, on each.

For a special attraction, ask guests to bring their most unusual Bibles for a Scripture display table. Award prizes for the most unique Bible, the oldest, the newest, the largest, the smallest, and the most obviously used. This is excellent publicity, as many newspapers will send a reporter to take pictures to highlight National Bible Week.

Menu

For a carry-in dinner, explain that each food must relate in some way to Scripture; for instance, Amos 8:1 mentions "a basket of ripe fruit." Each dish must be accompanied by its Scripture reference on a 3" x 5" card. This is a subtle way to start your congregation digging into their Bibles and concordances!

This activity is much easier than it sounds—Scripture abounds with food items. Little cakes (cupcakes?) are found in I Kings 17:13; corn, or grain, in Mark 4:28; cucumbers, or melons, in Isaiah 1:8; tender grapes, or figs, in the Song of Solomon 2:13, just to name a few. Lamb, meat, fowl, prunes, bread, and fruit are mentioned numerous times.

To simplify the dinner, you could select key passages that mention bread, meat, fruit, spices, and dainties, then arrange whatever food is brought under these five categories.

An ultra-easy menu could be a take-off of Jesus' feeding the five thousand with loaves and fishes. Stack up piles of tuna fish sandwiches, and you're home free!

There is one recipe that is an absolute must for inclusion in this dinner—Scripture Cake. The following is a version you'll want to try:

Scripture Cake

4½ cups I Kings 4:22 (flour)
1 cup each Judges 5:25 (milk and butter)
2 cups Jeremiah 6:20 (cane syrup)
2 tbsp. I Samuel 14:25 (honey)

2 cups Numbers 17:8 (almonds)	2 tsp. I Corinthians 5:6 (soda)
2 tsp. Amos 4:5 (baking powder)	2 tsp. Leviticus 2:13 (salt)
	6 Jeremiah 17:11 (eggs)
2 cups Nahum 3:12 (figs)	2 cups I Samuel 30:12 (raisins)

Mix like any fruit cake—whip the Judges, Jeremiah, and I Samuel 14:25 until light. Beat the 6 Jeremiah yolks and add to mixture. Add Kings, Amos, and Leviticus, alternating with Judges. Fold in Nahum, Numbers, and I Samuel 30:12, also 6 Jeremiah whites, beaten stiff. Season to taste with II Chronicles 9:9 (spices).

Line 13 x 9-inch pans with foil and bake in a moderate (300-325 degrees) oven for 1 hour. In greased 10-inch tube pans, bake for 2 hours. Serves 28.

This cake will be delicious because you have followed the recipe. The Bible is the same way. A friend may give you one; you may read it and think what it says seems logical or illogical, but you'll never know how good it is for your life unless you try the recipe.

Program

The mission organizations and Bible societies mentioned previously offer many excellent resources for program material on a free-will offering basis. Films, videos, cassettes, slides, and guest speakers are listed in free media brochures from most of these groups. A note of caution: Many of the films are booked well in advance of National Bible Week, so get your planning done early.

For a more informal program, choose Bible story pantomimes, Bible charades, quizzes, or Scripture trivia. Christian bookstores have fantastic assortments of Bible-related games, and your church librarian or pastor may also have Bible quiz books you can borrow.

A third alternative would be to have someone give a personal testimony of how God's Word has had a dramatic effect on his or her life. Most chapters of the Gideons International will direct you to people who have marvelous testimonies of how a Bible found in a hotel room drastically changed the course of their lives. Check the telephone directory for the number of your area Gideon representative.

Alternate ideas would be to present a brief history of Bible translations or to have a "walk through the Bible." Songs, such as "The B-I-B-L-E" or "Holy Bible, Book Divine," make inspired musical selections.

Devotions

Because this program revolves around Scripture, no separate devotional segment is required.

Other Events to Celebrate in November

- Everyone has favorite family traditions for Thanksgiving. Why not share yours by adopting a homeless family for the holiday? Or serve a free Thanksgiving dinner at church for all who want to come.

December

ARTS AND CRAFTS FAIR

No season of the year lends itself to family togetherness the way Christmas does. What family doesn't enjoy gathering around the kitchen table to crack nuts, create original decorations, or roll out Christmas cookies?

Very early in the season is a great time to give everyone in your church family an opportunity to share ideas at a holiday arts and crafts fair.

Decorations

No one ever tires of traditional holiday decor—greens, poinsettias, a tree, the works. For table centerpieces, ask families to bring something they have made for the holidays. You'll delight in seeing that nearly every family has something creative to share—pinecone centerpieces, baskets of holly, foam snowmen, crêches, driftwood decorated with holly and ivy.

Menu

Most of us are busy enough during the holidays, so keep the menu simple. A finger food supper saves a great deal of clean-up time; there is no silverware to wash! And finger foods are abundant, from celery and carrot sticks to pita bread sandwiches to egg rolls or fried won tons. Again, invite families to bring their favorite holiday finger foods, with a special emphasis on cheeseballs, cookies, and other specific holiday delicacies.

Program

Your program can be either simple or elaborate. For a simple program, in addition to the centerpieces and special foods, set up display tables in the narthex or at one end of your fellowship hall. Invite families to bring original Christmas arts and crafts, with directions for making them written on 3" x 5" cards. Give each participant a holiday-decorated notebook in which to copy down the items that appeal to his or her own talents or budget. Allow an hour or more for guests to circulate around the room, gathering ideas.

For a more structured program, invite several arts and crafts people to give how-to demonstrations, showing in detail how they made a particular craft. A small group could participate in a hands-on creative experience, duplicating the craft item.

To keep your program family oriented, ask all family members to explain or even to pantomime how they celebrate the holidays. A family cookie-making demonstration or mock shopping spree could bring down the house!

The following program includes a good assortment of music, humor, and information. It has been successfully adapted for use by large and small congregations.

Christmas Is for Families

PART I: TREASURES AND TRADITIONS

Have families perform or demonstrate the following scenes or have them present scenes from their own lives. (Note: The group could trim the tree during this segment, putting on the lights, ornaments, and star following each explanation.)

- The family that licks together sticks together; how to make—and send!—Christmas cards. (A demonstration by one family.)

- Papa Luther starts a tradition. (The story of Martin Luther's trek into the forest, resulting in history's first lighted Christmas tree.)

- Safari in the snow. (A church family tells of personal experiences in Christmas-tree hunting.)

- Let your light shine! (Information on how to care for and select tree lights.)

- "Fruity" advice. (Galatians 5:22-23, the fruit of the Spirit, which the bright glass ornaments represent on the tree.)

- I can do it myself! (A child demonstrates a particular ornament he or she has made.)

- *Fulguris, Fulguris, parva stella.* ("Twinkle, twinkle, little star"; a brief explanation of the wisemen and why we hang a star on the treetop.)

- An imp talks about angels. (A small child recites a piece about the Christmas angel and shows a treetop angel.)

- Putting on a good front. (An expert shows how to beautifully wrap a gift.)

- Please don't squeeze my wrapping paper! (A child demonstrates how to make wrapping paper, using newsprint roll, potato stencil, and stamp pad.)

- Give the best gift—yourself! (A parent suggests ways to give of yourself to others.)

- God's unspeakable gift. (The pastor or guest speaker gives a brief devotional about the advent of Christ.)

55

PART II: CUSTOMS AND CAROLS

During this segment, individuals can explain many of the traditional customs, such as bells, poinsettias, mistletoe, holly and ivy, candles, and Christmas seals. Intersperse with these customs group singing of appropriate carols; invite families to sing specific carols as musical specials, or invite a high school brass ensemble or orchestral group to provide special music.

Here's how one group planned this part of the program:

- Ghosts of Christmas Past (introduction)

- Ding, Dong, Avon Calling? (the custom of bells)

- "Evening Bells" (bell solo)

- "I Heard the Bells on Christmas Day" (group singing)

- Conserve electricity—Make Candles! (the custom of candle making)

- The Kissing Custom (the story of mistletoe)

- The Flower That's Not a Flower (the origin of the poinsettia)

- Seal It Up (the origin of Christmas seals)

- A Birthday Cake for Jesus (a small child sings "Happy Birthday" to Jesus)

- How to Enjoy Commercials—Turn 'em Off! (a family explains how station breaks during Christmas TV specials can be used to recite Bible verses, to give a special "love message" to a sibling, or to sing a carol)

- The Family That Sings Together Clings Together! (several family groups present special music)

- Talent Debut (two or three small children play musical selections, recital style)

- Night out with the Family (a father explains his family's custom of driving around to see the holiday decorations)

- Christmas Sing-along (carol singing)

- Here We Come a'Caroling (high school choral group strolls through the room, caroling)

- Hope for the Untalented! (an impromptu rhythm band performs, using instruments from the church nursery; a great way to include those who haven't as yet taken part in the program!)

- Instant Concert (high school brass or other instrumental ensemble)

PART III: FEASTING AND FELLOWSHIP

Close your program with one of these, and don't forget the Christmas eateries and punch afterward!

- Harried Homemakers (a brief and humorous declamation on how to keep your sanity during the Christmas rush)

- Someone's in the Kitchen with Mama (family cookie baking demonstration)

- Excruciating Headache No. 199 (a pantomime of a father's Christmas shopping experiences)

- I Will Not Scream at My Kids! (a young mother shares ideas on how to include little ones in the holiday preparations)

- The Greatest Story Ever Told (a family, with mother in rocking chair, sits in front of the Christmas tree while father reads the Christmas story; this is a poignant way to end the program)

The printed program can include a number of hints for a successful holiday. Leave room for guests to make notations or to sketch ideas. Some hints you may want to use are listed here.

Christmas Is for Worship

Candles for His Coming. Make a simple Advent wreath, consisting of four white candles with one red candle in the center. Four weeks before Christmas, on the first Sunday of Advent, the first candle is lit, symbolizing the joyful anticipation of Jesus' coming. A member of the family reads one of the prophecies concerning his coming while the candle burns.

Each Sunday during the month, one more candle is lit—on the second Sunday, two, the third, three, and so on. Enjoy Christmas stories, verses, and carols together. On Christmas Eve, after the four candles have been kindled, the fifth candle in the center is lit to remind the family of Jesus, the Light of the world. In the glow of candlelight, those in the home read the story of what happened in Bethlehem and rejoice in the coming of the Savior.

Family Card Party. Set aside one evening early in the season to design Christmas cards. Reminisce about the people on your list, praying for them as they come to mind. Meanwhile, keep little hands busy gluing strips of braid onto cards in the shape of candles, or green rick-rack and sequins for trees. Other family members can lick postage stamps and stuff envelopes. Be sure the cards you make will fit into standard-sized envelopes.

Tree-trimming Night. Make this a devotional time, with each family member taking part. Tell about Martin Luther's first Christmas tree and recite John 3:16 together as the tree is placed in its stand (the green representing our everlasting life). Sing "This Little Light of Mine" while stringing the lights.

Have someone read the angel's announcement to the shepherds as the angel is being fastened to the treetop. Explain that the ornaments represent the fruit of the Spirit, and have each person tell which fruit he or she wants most to display in life as each hangs an ornament on the tree. Finish off with tinsel and garland, representing the abundant life Jesus promises in John 10:10. This may not result in the most elegant tree on your block, but it will certainly be the most meaningful.

Christmas Is for Giving

A Secret Friend. Put names of all family members into a hat and draw a name. Be a secret friend to that person all month, doing special favors without that person finding out. Keep your identity a secret until Christmas morning.

Personal Presents. Make a gift for each one in your family. Our church family is full of ideas! Check idea books for suggestions.

Homemade Love. Give a gift straight from your kitchen. Fresh-baked cookies or homemade candy stacked in a decorated jar and tied with a bow really say, "We care."

Friends of the Elderly. Visit a shut-in, or adopt a grandparent. Area nursing homes are full of forgotten people. A short visit and a small gift from your family could really brighten someone's holiday. Or bring someone home for Christmas dinner.

A Penny Sent. Share some of your abundance. Place a bank under your tree and encourage family members to save money from their allowances to send to a missionary, to a Third World country, or to a favorite charity.

Christmas Is for Cooking!

Family Cookies. Here's a recipe for memorable Christmas cookies that get the whole family stirring!

Gather together: Mom, Dad, all the kids
Set: Dad to cracking nuts
    Kids to rolling out dough
    Mom to minding the oven
Stir in: Lots of good-natured kidding and mild horseplay
Keep: *Temper*ature moderate
    Timing slow (This recipe must not be rushed or hurried.)
Make: Allowances for messy countertops, a few shells in the nuts, and a dirty floor
Yield: Best-ever Christmas cookies, plus never-to-be-forgotten memories of a happy home

---

Easy Candy.

This is a recipe that even a child can make.

Blend together ⅓ cup evaporated milk with ½ cup peanut butter. Then stir in 2½ cups sifted confectioners' sugar. Knead this mixture until it is smooth. Roll out the dough and shape it into funny faces, using hard candies, chocolate pieces, coconut, and so on for decorations. No cooking, no baking, no failures!

Parting Thought

"Children have neither past nor future; they enjoy the present, which very few of us do."—La Bruyère, *Les Caractères*

Ideas for Simple Christmas Celebrations

- A tasting tea and recipe exchange is a welcome change from full-blown holiday dinners.

- To keep the calories under control, have an espresso-sipping party, complete with aerobic exercises.

Scripture-Based Programs

Passover

PASSOVER DINNER

The Jewish Passover coincides with the Christian Easter season on the church calendar. Because Christ was celebrating the Passover with his disciples when he initiated the Lord's Supper, or Holy Communion, many congregations like to have a Passover dinner on Maundy Thursday.

Whenever you choose to use it, the Passover dinner is a meaningful program for the entire church, Sunday school classes, women's or men's fellowship, or even for individual families. It is a time when all can sit around the table to appreciate the beauty of this most ancient Jewish holiday, while gaining understanding of the context of Holy Communion.

Jesus is linked so closely to Israel's Passover Feast that he is called "Christ our Passover lamb" in I Corinthians 5:7. The historical significance of this event, as told in Exodus, is meaningful to Christians and Jews alike, stemming from our common Old Testament heritage.

Decorations

A blue and white color scheme represents the Israeli flag. Decorate the tables simply, with white tablecloths and a blue streamer down the center, plus two white or blue candles on each table. The place settings for a *seder* (Passover) dinner require a great deal of space; hence the minimal table decorations. Items from the Holy Land placed about the room will add much to the atmosphere.

Playing tapes of inspirational Hebrew music will give a "Jewish flavor" to the evening. Many Messianic Jewish musical groups have recordings available.

The seder dinner must have a leader; therefore, proper table arrangement is important. The dinner works best with tables fanned out in a semicircle from the head table, giving everyone a view of the leader.

Set an extra place where no one will sit, complete with chair and place setting, at the head table, preferably closest to a door. This is "Elijah's place" and will be referred to during the service.

Fill a small cup with water and set it, along with a soup bowl and a small white towel or napkin, near the leader's place. During the service, the leader will ceremonially wash his or her hands by pouring water over them above the bowl and then wiping them off with the towel.

Prepare all tables with two candles, matches, a Unity (three pieces of *matzo*, unleavened bread, separated in a folded white napkin), a dinner plate of matzo (about one sheet of matzo per person), a bottle of grape juice, one six-ounce clear plastic cup per place setting, one very small cup of salt water per place setting, one sprig of parsley per place setting, and horseradish and *charoset* (a sweet mixture of apples and nuts) in small serving dishes to be passed around the table.

Menu

Since Orthodox Jewish tradition forbids eating meat and milk products at the same meal, cream and butter should not be served. Also, foods containing leaven (yeast) are taboo. Use matzo and its derivatives throughout the menu.

In areas of the country in which there is a large Jewish population, ingredients for the menu will be available at most food stores. If not, most food store managers can order the items for you. Or you could call a nearby synagogue for assistance in procuring the items.

The suggested menu includes:

Appetizers—chopped liver and/or gefilte fish and kosher pickles
Soup—chicken broth with matzo balls
Entree—roasted chicken
Vegetable—carrots or squash
Potato substitute—matzo stuffing
Bread substitute—only matzo is used
Dessert—sponge cake with fruit topping
Beverages—coffee (no milk or cream), hot or iced tea, grape juice (used in ceremonial portion)

Some of the foods used for a Passover dinner will seem strange and unfamiliar; however, you will discover that they are tasty. Have the cooks try the recipes for the main items at home before the actual dinner to familiarize themselves with them.

Charoset

1 cup peeled, chopped apples
¼ cup chopped walnuts
1 tsp. each honey and cinnamon
2 tbsp. grape juice
Grated rind of ½ lemon

Mix all ingredients. Add enough grape juice to blend the mixture. Approximate yield, one tablespoon per person, is 20 servings.

Chopped Liver

½ cup vegetable oil	2 hard-boiled eggs
2 medium onions, sliced	¾ tsp. salt
1 lb. chicken or beef liver	¼ tsp. pepper

Pour half of the oil into a skillet. Add the onions and sauté for about 10 minutes, then remove the onions and set them aside. Pour more oil in the skillet as needed. Sauté the liver for 10 minutes or until done, stirring occasionally. Chop onions, liver, and eggs very fine. Add seasonings and mix well. Chill. Form into one-inch balls, or you may wish to mold the mixture in a gelatin mold and serve it as one large portion per table.

Gefilte Fish

This is an ethnic delicacy for which most people have to acquire a taste. A tiny portion per person should be adequate. Buy the hors d'oeuvre size at the supermarket, and serve with matzo and horseradish.

Matzo Ball Soup

one 4 to 5 lb. chicken	2 sprigs parsley
3 qts. cold water	1 small bay leaf
1 sliced carrot	1 tbsp. salt
2 stalks celery and tops	¼ tsp. pepper

Cut the chicken into pieces. Place it in a large soup kettle with cold water; cover and bring it slowly to a boil. Add the seasonings and vegetables and simmer gently for about 5 hours. Strain the soup and chill it overnight. Remove the cake of fat and use it in stuffing and matzo ball recipes. Reheat the soup and add matzo balls for serving. This makes 2 quarts, or 8 servings. Add canned chicken broth to extend the recipe if needed.

Matzo Balls

2 tbsp. fat	1 tsp. salt
2 slightly beaten eggs	2 tbsp. soup stock or water
½ cup matzo meal	

Mix fat and eggs together. Mix together matzo meal and salt and add the mixture to the fat and eggs. When well blended, add soup stock or water. Cover the mixing bowl and place it in the refrigerator for at least 20 minutes. Then form the dough into 1½ inch balls. Using a 2- or 3-quart pot, bring salted water to a brisk boil. Reduce flame and drop the balls into the slightly bubbling water. Cover pot and cook 30 to 40 minutes.

Note: Matzo balls have a tendency to become very tough if mishandled, so work quickly. Matzo balls can be made several hours ahead of time. When preparing to serve, have soup at room temperature or warmer and remove matzo balls from water to soup pot. Allow soup to simmer for about five minutes. Makes 8 balls.

Roasted Chicken

For each five pounds of chicken quarters, place 1 large sliced onion, ½ cup diced celery, and 2 tbsp. melted chicken fat or margarine in a deep roaster.

Rub each chicken quarter with a mixture of 1 tsp. paprika, 1 tsp. salt, ¼ tsp. ground ginger, 1 tbsp. flour, and ¹/₁₆ tsp. garlic powder.

Place the chicken on the vegetables and roast uncovered for 20 minutes at 400 degrees. Turn the chicken over and roast 20 minutes longer. Lower the heat to 350 degrees and add ¾ cup boiling water for each 5 lbs. of chicken. Cover tightly and continue cooking until tender, about 1¼ hours.

Lemon Carrots

2 cups cooked carrots (fresh or frozen)
1 tsp. minced parsley
1 tsp. sugar
½ tsp. salt
½ tsp. paprika
1 tsp. lemon juice
1 tbsp. fat or butter

Drain the cooked carrots. While they are still hot, add remaining ingredients. Stir constantly over as low a heat as possible for 5 minutes, until each piece of carrot is coated with sauce. Serves 4.

Passover Stuffing

5 matzos
About 1 cup soup stock
2 eggs
4 tbsp. grated celery root or onion
pepper to taste
1 tbsp. chopped parsley
4 tbsp. chicken fat (from soup stock)
1 tsp. salt

Break up the matzos and moisten them in the soup stock. Let the mixture rest for 15 minutes. Beat the eggs and mix with remaining ingredients. Add this mixture to the matzo and mix well. Place in oiled pans and bake covered in 350 degree oven until done. Length of cooking time depends on the quantity baked. Figure one matzo per person.

Matzo Sponge Cake

9 eggs, separated
1⅓ cups sugar
6 tbsp. water
Juice and grated rind of 1 lemon
¾ cup matzo cake meal
¾ cup potato starch
pinch of salt

Beat egg yolks and water. Add sugar gradually and beat until very stiff. Add lemon juice and rind. Sift matzo cake meal, salt, and potato starch together and add gradually to egg yolks while beating very smooth. Beat egg whites until stiff. Fold into batter gently, but thoroughly. Turn into 10-inch tube pan. Bake in 325 degree oven for 1 hour and 10 minutes. Invert pan and let cool thoroughly before removing cake from pan.

Note: In some areas, kosher cake mixes or already baked kosher sponge cakes may be purchased.

Cakes may be topped with 1 cup raspberry jam, Danish junket or dessert mix, canned fruit thickened with potato starch, fresh fruit, such as strawberries, with sugar, or cut-up dried fruit simmered and thickened with potato starch.

Seder Plate Arrangement

The seder plate is the ceremonial setting for the first forty minutes of the service. It should be placed in front of the leader at the head table, or there can be one at each table of ten people. Included are items that will be partaken of to help the people better understand the meaning of the holiday.

Each plate should contain the *beytza* (roasted egg), *karpas* (sprig of parsley), *maror* (1 tsp. ground horseradish), *charoset* (1 tbsp. apples, nuts, and spices), one 2½ oz. cup of salt water (for dipping of *karpas*), and the *zeroah* (a shankbone of a lamb).

The salt water is placed in the center of the plate, with the other ingredients arranged clockwise, beginning at twelve o'clock with the horseradish. Parsley, shankbone, and *charoset* are spaced next, with the roasted egg ending the circle.

Program

Ideally, if your congregation wants an authentic Passover, complete with ceremonial service, it is best to invite a speaker from one of the Messianic mission agencies. The American Board of Missions to the Jews, P.O. Box 2000, Orangeburg, NY 10962 (telephone [914] 359-8535), can give you the name and address of a missionary in your vicinity. It also has available a Passover kit, with complete, detailed instructions for giving your own dinner.

Using this dinner to celebrate the Lord's Last Supper is also effective, skipping the Jewish ceremonial portions but serving the Christian Communion after supper. The film *Christ in the Passover* is effective when used with this dinner. It is available from the above mission agency.

The actual Passover dinner and traditional service in the Jewish home take about six hours. The following is an abbreviated version, which focuses on the key themes of Passover and serves as an effective bridge between the Old and the New Testaments.

Christ in the Passover

Introduction: Tonight, as we go through an abbreviated Passover service, we will point out the memorial aspect of the Passover to the Jewish nation, and also how the Passover foretells of the Messiah—Jesus Christ. We'll see how his Last Supper really was a Passover Seder and gain tremendous insight into the Lord's Supper.

The Search for Leaven: Called the *Bedikath Hametz*, the search for leaven begins several days before the first evening of Passover. The mother and daughters do a thorough house cleaning, ridding the house of all leaven, fulfilling the biblical command that there should be no leaven found in the house during the Passover season. Cakes, cookies, breads, and anything containing yeast or leavening must go.

In the New Testament, the apostle Paul likens leaven to sin in the life of a Christian. As the Jewish home is symbolically cleansed of leaven before celebrating Passover, the Christian's life is to be free of the leaven of sin before he or she participates in the Lord's Supper.

Hymn: "Cleanse Me" (or other hymn of confession)

Lighting of the Candles: Before the meal begins, the mother lights the seder candles and recites the blessing. (At this point, a "mother" should be selected at each table to light the candles.) Just as at the beginning of the Jewish Passover the woman brings light into the darkness, we note that the Messiah, who came to bring light into the darkness of this world, was born of woman.

Hymn: "The Light of the World Is Jesus"

The Kiddush Cup, or Cup of Blessing: In Jewish tradition, the *Kiddush*, or blessing, begins most religious ceremonies; it sets the evening apart unto the Lord. (Point out to the people that each of them has a small cup in front of them. Explain that this cup will be drunk from four times during the evening, twice before the actual meal and twice after.)

The "father" at each table pours the first cup of wine and recites this blessing: "Blessed art thou, O Lord our God, Ruler of the World, Creator of the fruit of the grapevine." All then drink the first cup, while leaning to the left. This is a reminder that on this night they were freed from bondage in Egypt and, therefore, can relax as they eat.

The Urchatz, or Washing of the Hands: For this ceremony, the leader at the head table will ceremonially wash his hands by pouring water from a small container over his hands into a bowl. He then wipes his hands with the towel, signifying he is clean and ready to proceed with the ceremony. It was at this point in the Last Supper that Jesus washed his disciples' feet. This is a good place to read John 13:1-17.

The Karpas, or Eating a Green Vegetable: The "fathers" at each table will take the seder plate, locate the parsley, or karpas, break off a sprig, and dip it into the salt water. Each person at the table should do the same. Before everyone eats the salt-dipped karpas, the leader recites, "Blessed art thou, O Lord our God, Ruler of the world, Creator of the fruit of the earth."

Yachatz, the Afikoman: On each table has been placed a napkin containing three pieces of matzo. Each matzo is separated from the others by a fold in the napkin, but all are contained in one napkin. On top of this you will find another napkin folded in half. The "father" at each table will pull out the middle piece of matzo, break it into two pieces, put the larger piece of broken matzo back in the middle, and take the other piece and wrap it in the napkin that was on top of the pile of three. The piece that has been wrapped is now called the *afikoman* and should be hidden by the "father" someplace around the table.

This ceremony has special significance to the Christian. The three pieces of unleavened bread in one container, one yet separate, called the *echod*, or "Unity," clearly represent the Trinity—one God, manifesting himself as Father, Son, and Holy Spirit. You will notice that the middle matzo, representing the Son, is taken from the Unity and is broken. A portion is returned to the Unity, while the other half is wrapped in a linen napkin and buried away. What a beautiful portrayal of Christ, who left his home in heaven, yet did not cease to be God. His human body was broken for us, wrapped in linen grave clothes, and buried!

The Maggid, the Passover Story: At this point, the Jewish family retells the historical saga of the Passover, reading from Exodus 12.

The Second Cup, or Cup of Praise: The second cup of wine is poured, and the leader recounts the plagues. As each plague is read off, each person dips his or her little finger into the cup of juice, pulls out a drop, and shakes it onto his or her plate. The plagues are: blood, boils, frogs, hail, lice, locusts, flies, darkness, cattle blight, and the slaying of the first born.

This is a time of great praise and thanksgiving in the Jewish home, a time when many happy choruses are sung. Your group may wish to sing "Alleluia" or some other song of praise.

Pesah, or Shankbone: The leader lifts the shankbone of the lamb from his seder plate, explaining that it represents the Passover lamb, which was used as a sacrifice in the days of the Temple. Since there is no longer a Temple, there cannot be any sacrifice. Thus Jewish families do not serve lamb at their Passover meal. Christians know that the final, ultimate sacrifice was the Messiah, the Lamb of God, who came to "take away the sins of the world."

The Matzo: Each "father" lifts up the plate of matzos (not the Unity), while the leader explains the reason for eating unleavened bread (Exodus 12:15-20). All eat together a small piece of matzo.

The Maror: The "father" points out the bitter herbs, or horseradish, on the seder plate. The leader explains that these represent the bitterness that the children of Israel suffered at the hands of the Egyptians. Each person dips a tiny picce of matzo into the bitter herbs and eats it. This is to bring tears to their eyes, to remind them of the many tears shed by the Jews when they were in slavery. This is a good place to discuss our freedom in Christ.

The Hallel: Everyone now raises the previously poured cup of wine while the blessing is recited by the leader: "Blessed art Thou, O Lord our God, Ruler of the world, Creator of the fruit of the earth." No one drinks yet. Psalms 113 and 114 are read responsively. The second cup of wine is then drunk.

The Korekh: The "father" at each table gives two pieces of broken matzo to each person. On this they place a small portion of horseradish and some of the *charoset* to form a miniature sandwich. This is called "Hillel's Sandwich," because Rabbi Hillel, who lived around the time of Christ, said that this sandwich represented life. The matzo represents the staff of life.

As one goes through life, one encounters two situations: bitterness (the horseradish) and sweetness (the charoset). One must learn to live with both if one is to be happy. All eat together of the "Hillel Sandwich."

The Beytza, or Egg: The leader points out the one untouched item on the seder plate, the boiled egg. It represents sacrifice for the sins of the people in the days of the Temple.

At this point the ceremonial part of the Passover is interrupted and the actual dinner is served. While the group is eating, the "fathers" may want to more securely hide the afikoman, the piece of matzo that was wrapped in the napkin. Be sure to play Hebrew background music during the meal.

The Third Cup, or Cup of Redemption: Immediately after dessert, the third cup of wine is poured, but not drunk. The children search for the matzo the "fathers" hid. Once it is found, it is returned to the "father," who "redeems" it with a coin. The "father" takes the redeemed piece of matzo, breaks it into small pieces, and distributes a piece to each person at the table.

Luke 22:20 points out that it was this third cup, the "cup after supper" which Jesus used when he declared, "This cup which is poured out for you is the new covenant in my blood" (RSV). How fitting that the Jewish "Cup of Redemption" is one and the same as the cup of our redemption, which we celebrate during Holy Communion!

You may want to explain that, to the Jewish people, the afikoman is the final dessert of the Passover meal, considered to be the substitute for the Paschal lamb. But to the Christian, the afikoman means something more. The word, translated from the Greek, means "I have come!" This is most likely the piece of bread that our Lord took in the upper room, which he said represented his body, which was broken for us. In other words, the Lord lifted the Cup of Redemption from the Jewish Passover and initiated a new covenant with us—the communion, or cup of the New Testament.

The third cup is now blessed and drunk together.

Fourth Cup, or Cup of Elijah: One Passover custom is to set a special place for Elijah. This place is left vacant in the hope that Elijah will appear during the evening. At the close of the evening, all the children scurry to the door, looking up and down the street for Elijah. They return, looking downcast and forlorn, reporting that Elijah is nowhere to be found. The parents, in an effort to console the children, comfort them with the words, "Maybe next year in Jerusalem!" Likewise, the Christian is looking for the second coming of the Messiah.

Psalms 113–118 are read. The Christian will recognize these as Messianic psalms, prophetic scriptures about Christ. Note especially Psalm 118:22, which the apostle Peter alludes to in I Peter 2:8 as being descriptive of Christ.

The Hymn: Following the Last Supper, according to the scripture, the disciples sang a hymn. The Jewish family also sings a song at the conclusion of the Passover meal. Any hymn of praise will fit nicely here.

Leader: The seder of Passover is now complete, even as our salvation and redemption are complete in Jesus Christ. As Christ said from the cross, "It is finished." There is absolutely nothing we can do to add to the glorious fact that our salvation is complete in him. Maybe next year in the New Jerusalem!

Manna

MEAL OF MANNA

When they were starving in the wilderness, the children of Israel complained against God and Moses. To still their complaints, God sent them food in the form of a small white thing spread upon the ground. Not knowing what kind of food this was, the Israelites called it *manna*, which literally means, "What is it?"

Satisfy the hunger pangs in your group and enjoy a few jokes with a meal of "What is it?"—manna. Serving mystery manna is a super way to clean out the refrigerator and pantry on the last day of camp, to feed the crew at a church clean-up day, or simply to have a fun-filled inexpensive party.

Decorations

Transform your fellowship hall into a biblical wilderness by importing cacti, boxes of sand, and makeshift tents. Clothespins turned Israelites, potted cacti, or miniature stone "tablets" serve as centerpieces. Use burlap or grasscloth for table coverings.

For a simpler decor, use flannelgraph or wilderness pictures from your Sunday school files.

Menu

For manna, have every family in the church bring its version of Stockpot Soup, Sunday Leftover Surprise, or Recycled Refrigerator Refugees. In other words, anything that will evoke the "What is it?" query that teenagers and children invariably ask when confronted with a stew-like concoction.

Set pots or baskets full of broken bread or crackers on each table. Any leftovers qualify as ingredients for future manna!

Program

Play charades, using events from Exodus and the wilderness wanderings, or assign each class, group, or family a part of the wanderings to act out in a skit. If available, show a filmstrip on the wanderings.

For more fun, have everyone dress as Israelites on the move. If you're using printed programs, phrase every section with the "Thou shalts" of the Ten Commandments.

Devotions

Use Scripture readings that show how God cares for his children, or read the story about the gift of manna in Exodus 16.

Deuteronomy 32:7

DOWN MEMORY LANE

Deuteronomy 32:7 reminds us to "remember the days of old, consider the years of many generations" (KJV). Homecomings, family or church reunions, anniversary parties, or mortgage burning celebrations all offer great opportunities to walk down memory lane. Or how about a special dinner to honor your congregation's senior citizens or charter members?

Decorations

Old-fashioned quilts used as tablecloths provide a fantastic backdrop for centerpieces of hurricane lamps, pitcher and bowl sets, crocheted flowers set in crocks or tea kettles, or antique gadgets artfully arranged. Use larger antiques, such as butter churns, washboards, or rug beaters, to highlight the head table.

Nut cups made from foil-covered spray-container lids and miniature washboards will bring back memories of Grandma's washday. The washboards are easily created from tiny pieces of cardboard glued to two craft sticks. For another unusual and amusing party favor, make tiny outhouses from rough wood. Use them later as penny banks.

Anything that's old will further add to the decor. Display

Grandma's cookbooks, family Bibles, or old photo albums for a tremendous center of interest.

Menu

Recipes that Grandma used are the order of the day. Try apple butter, homemade cookies, biscuits, Virginia baked ham—only "scratch" recipes here! Or why not freeze authentic homemade ice cream for a real old-fashioned ice cream social?

Old-Fashioned
Virginia Spoon Bread

6 cups white cornmeal
4 qts. milk
2 doz. eggs
½ cup butter or margarine
3 tbsp. salt

Put cornmeal into large kettle; add milk. Mix thoroughly and cook over medium heat until mixture thickens, stirring constantly. Remove from heat. Separate eggs. Beat whites until stiff; then beat yolks until thick and lemon-colored. Add yolks to cornmeal mixture; add butter and salt. Blend well; then fold in egg whites. Pour into 4 ungreased 9 x 13 baking pans. Bake at 350 degrees for 45-55 minutes. Serve with spoons. Makes 50 servings.

Program

A black silhouette of an antique oil lamp on beige paper makes a terrific old-looking program cover. Your program, itself, will depend on the occasion. An antique gadget demonstration goes over well, as does a fashion show featuring old-fashioned bathing suits, gowns, or hats. It's also fun for an honest-to-goodness octogenarian to tell how she made lye soap, to give the history of the area, to tell a little about the "good old days," or perhaps to recall the highlights of your church's history.

For youth parties, dig up old snapshots or slides of events in the kids' lives, unbeknownst to them, and have a surprise presentation.

Devotions

A song that fits the occasion is "Precious Memories." Psalm 77:11-12 picks up the mood of memories, or your speaker may wish to focus on the verse in Deuteronomy.

Variations

This theme is also good for honoring a retiring pastor or as a farewell to an active family that is moving away. If an individual is to be honored, a "This Is Your Life" program can be presented, along with a memory book with pictures and addresses of local friends. For a really special person, church members may want to fashion a friendship quilt, with each person or family designing one quilt square.

Psalm 23

A SHEPHERD'S DINNER

The quiet, serene security of Psalm 23, the Shepherd Psalm, comes alive in this theme. It can be adapted for any luncheon or dinner and is suitable for any age group—the Twenty-third Psalm is universally loved!

Pastors are often called "undershepherds of the flock," so this would be especially appropriate for an ordination or installation dinner, or as a pastor-appreciation banquet.

Decorations

Surround oval or round mirrors with small rocks, flowers, and "trees" (tiny branches stuck in modeling clay) to form the centerpieces—miniature lakes or "still waters." Miniature sheep, borrowed from nativity sets or from children's toy farms or made of balls of white cotton or craft foam, cavort near the lake. Sheep patterns are available in nearly all nursery and beginner Sunday school teachers' aid packets for the spring quarter each year.

Lean shepherds' crooks, or staffs, against the wall for more atmosphere, or display old-fashioned sling shots. If you know any black-powder buffs, borrow their powder horns to hang on the wall, too.

Spring-green tablecloths resemble the "green pastures." These are usually available at most discount shopping stores, or you can borrow someone's light-green sheets for table covers.

Menu

Ask members of your women's circle to bring a casserole of their favorite Shepherd's Pie recipe. Then add hot rolls and a green salad to "prepare the table before you." A white coconut cake shaped like a lamb makes an adorable centerpiece for your buffet table and also serves as dessert. Lamb cake patterns are available at most cake decorating stores and in cake decorating books.

Roast leg of lamb with all the trimmings would be a good choice for a more formal banquet.

Program

Ordination, installation, or appreciation dinners would include testimonials, speakers, and appropriate music, in a more-or-less prescribed program. Good music choices include: "Savior, Like a Shepherd Lead Us," "The New 23rd," "The Lord Is My Shepherd," "Surely, Goodness and Mercy," or the more formal "He Shall Feed His Flock."

Several excellent flannelgraph lessons and flip-chart books on the Shepherd Psalm are available at most Christian bookstores. These take care of the program for a children's or family dinner using this theme. Shepherd songs for children include the round "The Lord Is My Shepherd." You may want to try new words to the well-known "He Invites Me to His Banqueting Table" (for example, "We are the sheep and he is the shepherd, His banner over us is love").

Children also love to play games, such as "Run, Sheep, Run," "Ring the Shepherd's Staff" (fruit jar rings tossed at the crook, ring-toss fashion), or "Fox and Sheep" (a variation of the familiar fox and goose game).

Devotions

Devotions will be an integral part of the main program in most cases, but will certainly center on Psalm 23. Another good passage dealing with sheep is John 10. A formal speaker may want to focus on the Good Shepherd of Psalm 23, the Great Shepherd of Hebrews 13:20, and the Chief Shepherd of I Peter 5:4.

Variations

The Twenty-third Psalm is used at many funerals to bring comfort to the bereaved. Many churches are discovering the ministry of serving a dinner either before or after a funeral to families and friends of the deceased. In small towns, neighbors and friends usually bring casseroles, and the serving group has to furnish only rolls and beverages. The most important thing is to provide a quiet, restful atmosphere where people can be together as a family before they travel back to their homes. Simple flower arrangements on white or pastel tablecloths are the only decorations needed.

Ecclesiastes 3

TIME PASSAGES

Father Time has long been the subject of moans and groans. It seems people never have enough time, or they have too much time on their hands, or they wonder where the time has gone.

Get your clocks going on the right track from Daylight Savings to Standard Time with a "Timely Dinner." Or set the timer for a New Year's Eve party. Or put prophecy in perspective for a prophecy conference.

Decorations

Clocks and timepieces of any shape, size, and tone tick away at centerstage. Calendars—futuristic, antique, or foreign—can adorn the walls, while miniature sundials, hourglasses, mantel clocks, and pocket watches serve as centerpieces. Talking about these displays of unusual clocks and watches will help people "while away the time" as they wait for the program to begin.

Menu

Like time, food is at a premium and shouldn't be wasted. Before all those leftovers in the refrigerator become throw-outs, have everyone concoct creative and innovative dishes from the leftovers they have on hand. Leftover mashed potatoes make terrific mashed potato pancakes, for instance.

Another idea is to have sandwiches made on day-old bread or recipes mentioning time, such as "Five-Minute Fudge."

Five-Minute Fudge

6 oz. evaporated milk
1⅔ cups sugar
½ tsp. salt
½ cup chopped walnuts
1½ cups diced marshmallows
1½ cups semisweet chocolate pieces
1 tsp. vanilla

Grease a 9" x 9" x 1¾" pan. In a medium saucepan, combine the evaporated milk with sugar and salt and bring to a boil. Reduce heat and simmer, stirring constantly for 5 minutes. Remove from heat. Add remaining ingredients, stirring until marshmallows melt. Pour into prepared pan; let cool. To serve, cut into squares.

Program

If you are using a printed program, design it in the form of a time schedule. Round, smiling clock faces make cute name tags. Or use verses from Ecclesiastes 3 to designate each part of the program ("There is a time for everything"). Set alarm clocks to ring in each segment of the program.

Have a Bible drill, using verses with references to time. Set Ecclesiastes 3 to music, with slides to illustrate each point. Songs such as "I Know Who Holds the Future" or "I Was in His Mind" would be . . . timely!

Devotions

Discuss prophecy, past and future, or have a discussion of Ecclesiastes 3.

Variations

This theme adapts well for a "Prime Time" party for senior citizens. Use it as a senior retreat, Sunday school class dinner, or senior citizens' center dinner. Have a speaker discuss ways to get the most out of life at any age, including proper nutrition, exercise, and mental attitude.

Song of Solomon

SOLOMON'S LOVE GARDEN

The romantic in all of us takes exquisite delight in the expression of pure marital love given us by King Solomon. This theme especially lends itself to a couples' Sunday school class party, to a bridal shower, to an engagement party, to a wedding reception, or perhaps as a closing banquet for a marriage encounter weekend.

Decorations

The more you can make your premises resemble a lovely garden, the better the atmosphere will be. The Song of Solomon mentions a number of flowers—lily of the valley, rose of Sharon, apple blossoms. In verse 9 of chapter 2, the lover looks through a lattice. Why not construct a lattice arbor, lavishly covered with silk or paper roses?

The smell of elegant spices would be delicious, as mentioned in the Song of Solomon 4:14. An ambitious decorating committee may even want to install the fountain mentioned in verse 15 of chapter 4.

Centerpieces could be bowls of apples, grapes, and figs or floral displays of roses and lilies. Handmade spice balls would make nice favors and would add to the pleasant aromas.

Miniature birds, available at florist shops, could be wired to blooming apple tree branches and used as the centerpiece on the speaker's table.

Menu

How about sticking to a purely vegetarian menu for this one? For a garden party in the right season, folks will enjoy bringing some of the fruits of their labor. Corn, green beans, peas, potatoes, salads, squash—whatever happens to be in season will make a delightful and healthful meal. Dessert could be apple or berry pies. Solomon mentions honey a number of times in his love message. You may want to serve scones and honey with your vegetables.

A wedding reception or bridal shower traditionally calls for wedding cake, punch, nuts, and mints. You can tie these foods into the theme by decorating them with lilies, roses, and apple blossoms.

Scones

2 cups buttermilk	1¼ tsp. salt
1 large egg	¾ tsp. baking pow-
3 tbsp. vegetable oil	der
1 tbsp. sugar	¼ tsp. baking soda
1 package active dry	oil for deep-fat frying
yeast	
5–6 cups all-purpose	
flour	

Heat buttermilk until bubbles form at edge of pan. Set aside to cool. When buttermilk has cooled to 110 degrees F, stir in egg, oil, sugar, and yeast until well mixed; set aside for five minutes until yeast softens.

In mixing bowl, stir together 5 cups flour, salt, baking powder, and soda. Make a well in the center of the flour mixture; pour buttermilk mixture into well. Stir until soft dough forms, adding more flour as needed. Knead dough about 10 times on lightly floured surface. Invert bowl over dough and let rise about 30 minutes or until double in size.

Heat cooking oil in large, heavy skillet (about 1–2 inches deep). When a drop of water sizzles (375 degrees F), the oil is ready for frying.

Shape dough into 1⅓ inch balls. Roll dough balls to 3½ inch rounds on lightly floured surface. Fry in batches, turning once to brown both sides (about 2 minutes per side). Drain on paper towels and serve warm with honey butter (Makes 32 scones.).

Honey Butter

Mix 1 pound soft margarine with 1 cup honey and spread over scones.

Program

A good reader could present selected portions of the Song of Solomon. This beautiful love poem is even more dramatic when a man and a woman read the respective parts. Many Bibles, such as the Good News Bible, have the different voices clearly defined.

For guest speakers, you may want to invite a couple in your church who have celebrated their fiftieth wedding anniversary.

This would also be a good occasion to view the film *Strike the Original Match,* by Charles Swindoll, or to check out some of the other marital offerings at your local library or other film supplier.

The familiar chorus, "He Invites Me to His Banqueting Table," is a must, since it is based on the Song of Solomon 2:4.

Many churches have discovered the joy of having couples repeat and renew their wedding vows en masse. During this banquet would be a great time for such a renewal.

Matthew 4:18-22

FISHERS OF MEN

Anyone who has ever dangled a baited hook in a stream has at least one good fish tale to cast upon any available ear! Give your fishing enthusiasts an excuse to spin their tales at a fish feast.

A father and son outing, a church campout, or the preparation for an evangelistic outreach would all be a good reason for a "Fishers of Men" feed.

Decorations

Drape the walls and ceiling with fish net and spangle the net with starfish, shells, pieces of driftwood, and dried seaweed. Newspaper laid out flat on the tables provides inexpensive fish-and-chips style tablecloths. For centerpieces, cast about for fishing poles, reels, and tackle boxes brimming with flies, hooks, and lines.

Menu

If you've actually gone fishing, simply have a fish fry with everyone cooking up the catch of the day. Or serve fish and chips in newspaper wrappers reminiscent of the old fish markets. To evoke memories of Jesus' feeding the multitudes, place baskets of barley loaves or other breads on the tables.

Program

This is the chance to swap fish stories. Give a rusty hook to the person with the wildest story. Award an old-fashioned fishing pole, a string tied to a stick, to the person with the zaniest fishing hat. You also can give a prize for the biggest one that got away or for the most bizarre catch. Sing songs such as the children's chorus "I Will Make You Fishers of Men," or any songs about the sea, about ships, or about a lighthouse, such as "I Thank God for the Lighthouse."

Devotions

If this program precedes an evangelistic outreach, use scriptures, such as Matthew 4:18-22, to show that God wants us to be "fishers of men."

You could also enact or tell the story of Jesus' feeding the multitude in Matthew 14:15-21, Mark 6:32-44, or Luke 9:12-17.

Variations

Use this idea for an "Anglers' Breakfast" on the first day of fishing season—before heading out to the lakes and streams. Serve sour-dough pancakes, sausage, and scrambled eggs to get the day off to a good start.

Missions

"GO YE" BANQUET

This international food fair with a flair is excellent for a missionary conference, a missionary commissioning service, or a "One Great Hour of Sharing" kick-off dinner.

Decorations

Ask the people in your group to bring anything and everything they have from a foreign country. Be ready for total culture shock! You will be bombarded with everything from Swiss music boxes to Mexican sombreros to Japanese chopsticks. One ambitious group even decorated a cake to look like a Japanese car.

All these foreign trinkets can be arranged as centerpieces, grouping them according to country or continent. A word of caution: Don't use soilable items, such as an Israeli prayer shawl, on tables on which folks will be eating. Hang such items from the wall, drape them over the piano, or display them on a special table.

The head table could display a large globe surrounded by tiny flags of different countries (available at stationery stores or copied from an encyclopedia). Dress clothespin dolls in ethnic clothing and group them around the globe.

Cover the walls with large flags, maps, or calendar pictures of other countries. You may want to feature only those countries in which your church has missionaries; you may include enlarged photos of those missionaries as well.

Menu

With the boom in ethnic foods here in the United States, menu planning for this dinner is a snap. If you're having a potluck, your only rule needs to be, "Bring a foreign food!"

Pita bread sandwiches, pizza, pasta of any kind, tacos, chili, Yorkshire pudding, chow mein, Belgian waffles, French bread—did it ever occur to you that most of the food we eat didn't originate here?

For a unique twist, keep the menu a secret. Then serve each guest with a glass of water and a few grains of wheat. The money that would have been spent for food can be given to a Third World country's hunger center. Your guests will go away hungry, but it makes an unforgettable object lesson. This "dinner" is particularly effective for a "One Great Hour of Sharing" type of offering.

Program

Here's the place for an interesting missionary slide program, an American Bible Society film, or a full-length movie on missions (usually available free of charge from your church's mission agencies). Or contact a faith mission organization, such as TEAM (The Evangelical Alliance Mission), P.O. Box 969, Wheaton, Illinois 60189.

Written by an unknown author, the following words, sung to the familiar hymn "How Great Thou Art," have an excellent missionary message:

Until They Know

Oh, when I think of all the many millions
Who do not know the sound of Thy sweet name,
Who do not know the miracle of Calvary,
Who never can Thy great salvation claim,

Then cries my heart, "O teach me Lord to care,
Until they know how great Thou art!"
Then cries my heart, "O teach me Lord to care,
Until they know how great Thou art!"

Oh, when I think of all the heathen idols,
Those lifeless gods, just made of wood and stone.
And when I think of people calling to them—
Deaf ears that cannot hear the heart-sick groan,
Then cries my heart, "O make us go and tell
Of Jesus whom we love so well."
Then cries my heart, "O make us go and tell
Of Jesus whom we love so well."

But when they know that Jesus died to save them
And when they know the grace He can impart.
When Jesus shines His love divine within them;
When He transforms their sinful, darkened heart:
Then they shall sing, my Savior God to Thee,
"How great Thou art! How great Thou art!"
Then they shall sing, my Savior God to Thee,
"How great Thou art! How great Thou art!"

Devotions

Scripture readings and the devotional message could center around Matthew 28:19-20, Acts 1:8, or other great missions passages.

Church History

THE CHURCH'S ONE FOUNDATION

There's no better time than a church ground-breaking, church dedication, church mortgage burning, or church reunion to recall the history of this particular congregation and the biblical principles of the church universal. This theme would also work for a church spruce-up day or for honoring a retiring pastor or charter member.

Decorations

Dust off the church photo album and have enlargements made of some of the more notable events in the church's history. Arrange these photos prominently around the room. Try to get old newspaper stories of precious church events; plaster these on the walls or on bulletin boards.

Deck the tables with plain newsprint or white paper cloths and draw blueprints or floorplans on them. As centerpieces, arrange hand tools or pieces of material used to build the church. You might even want to have a display of work shoes, overalls, or carpenters' aprons to symbolize those worn during the original construction of the church. Old invoices, bills of lading, or land sales papers will make intriguing reading and animated conversation when your guests find them among the tools on the tables.

If you are celebrating the building of a new church, be sure to invite those who helped with construction—contractors, subcontractors, and volunteer workers.

Menu

Using the construction idea, lay out all the makings for hoagie or deli sandwiches and let each person "build" his or her own dinner.

Or "construct" a salad supper, with the only rule being that everyone must bring some kind of salad. To ensure variety, you may want to assign meat salads, vegetable salads, green salads, gelatin salads, and dessert salads. Or have everyone bring a supply of one item for a salad.

Program

Show slides or home movies of your congregation's history or ask a charter member to relate some of the more interesting events in the life of the church. Don't overlook the abundance of special-events photos available—wedding pictures, baptismal photos, anniversaries. You'll be amazed at how many folks have pictures that were taken at your church.

Many denominations offer filmstrips or films on their particular historical backgrounds. You may want to get a film on the life of some great church leader, such as Martin Luther or John Wesley.

To honor a special person, use a "This Is Your Life" approach.

Devotions

Sing "The Church's One Foundation" and use I Corinthians 3 or I Peter 2 as background to talk about Christ's great "building," the church.

Matthew 5

LOVE FEAST

In the New Testament church, the early believers shared a "Love Feast" before partaking of the Lord's Supper. People brought what they could to share with their brothers and sisters in the Lord.

Show your group's love and unity by having a modern love feast to help a needy family or disaster victims, to raise money for a sick member, or to welcome a new pastor. The object is for members to share what God has blessed them with, be it clothing, food, money, household items, or some talent or skill.

Decorations

Keep the focus on the need at hand. If money is being raised or food donated, place banks or small boxes on the tables for the donations. These will serve as your centerpieces.

At each place setting, put a small placard with one of the Beatitudes (Matthew 5) written on it, or set bookmarks inscribed with the Beatitudes at each place.

Slogans such as "Sharing Is Caring" can be made into colorful wall banners, or you can display posters with Bible verses, pictures of banquet tables, or photos of children sharing.

Menu

This should be a true carry-in, with each family bringing its best-tasting recipe.

Program

Use this time to explain the need at hand or to introduce the new pastor and his or her family. If the event is designed to raise money for a needy family that your church is supporting overseas, share pictures of the family and letters from the family members.

Devotions

Read the Beatitudes from Matthew 5 or Luke 20:20-49. Play soft music during the reading and use slides or a filmstrip to depict the people mentioned in the Beatitudes. For example, a ghetto scene would help to portray the poor; a picture of starving children would depict the hungry; a mother crying over a dead child would show those who mourn, and so on.

Other Ways to Share

A love feast would also be a good time to restock the church or community food bank for the needy. A contest could be held between various Sunday school classes, youth groups, and so forth to see who can furnish the most canned goods in a given time. Then recognize the winning team at a love feast.

I Corinthians 16:9

A GREAT DOOR FOR EFFECTIVE WORK

In I Corinthians 16:9, the Apostle Paul speaks of a "great door for effective work." To most of us, an open door represents opportunity; therefore, use this theme for any occasion when you want to stress golden opportunities—careers day, church groundbreaking, installation of officers, missionary commissioning service.

Decorations

Create a large paper or sheet backdrop with a large knocking hand outlined on it. Print or pin on it the last part of Matthew 7:7: "Knock and the door will be opened to you." The famous picture of Christ knocking at a heart's door would also be a fine display. Or you might print, perhaps in calligraphy or other decorative lettering, the many Scripture references to doors and place these about the room: "I am the door," from John 10, for instance.

Centerpieces could be door knockers, doorknobs, large keys, or cardboard doors with easels glued to their backs.

Menu

Open-faced sandwiches, relish trays, and simple desserts are suggested for an informal meal.

If you want a full-scale banquet, lock in on your human resources for ideas. Nearly every group has someone who works or has worked in the food service industry—a retired military cook, a school or institutional food service employee, a restaurant owner or worker, or a home economics teacher. Tap their experience for menu ideas, and then ask those same persons to participate in the program. They could give cooking demonstrations, tell how God helps in their careers, or discuss career possibilities in the food service industry.

Program

The program will depend on the occasion. A careers day program could include a panel discussion by several people who are successful in different fields; perhaps you might include a doctor, a teacher, a police officer, a cook, and a factory worker. One of those same people could be asked to speak on a particular career choice. "How I Serve God in My Job," "How God Directed Me into This Field," or "Career Opportunities in My Field" are possible topics.

A groundbreaking ceremony or installation of officers would require a more traditional program, but its emphasis could be on "Open Doors." In a commissioning service for a missionary, the honoree could tell what opportunities of service are ahead or how God has opened the doors leading up to this moment.

Devotions

First Corinthians 16:9, John 10, or Matthew 7:7-8 will all suggest suitable "doors" for discussion.

Ephesians 6

PUT ON THE FULL ARMOR OF GOD

All Christians are advised to "put on the full armor of God." This theme works equally well for a woman's banquet, a father-son event, an athletic awards banquet, a dinner honoring those in the military, or a youth supper.

Decorations

Use a blue, gold, and silver color scheme. Yellow table covers look stunning when accented with aluminum foil runners down the center. Taking your cue from Ephesians 6:11-18, create centerpieces to represent the various parts of the Christian's armor.

The belt of truth surrounds a blue vase of yellow flowers for one table. The belt can be any ordinary belt wide enough to glue on the letters T-r-u-t-h. Or search out a water skier's safety belt or a karate black belt.

For another table, feature a down-filled ski vest or a life-preserver vest with a blue ribbon emblazoned across it. The words "Breastplate of Righteousness" shimmer on the ribbon in gold glitter.

"Fitting the feet with the gospel of peace" is as simple as tucking a few yellow and blue flowers into an old pair of hiking boots or football, golf, bowling, gym, or snow shoes—whatever best suits your theme. Again, drape with blue ribbon, proclaiming "Peace" in glitter.

The shield of faith takes a little more ingenuity. Make a small cardboard shield. Cover it with foil and stripe it with a blue ribbon with the message "Faith" printed in glitter.

The helmet of salvation can be a football helmet, a motorcycle helmet, or a baseball cap. Fill it with flowers and bedeck it with the word "Salvation" in gold glitter on a blue ribbon.

The sword of the Spirit can be placed on the head table. Use a large pulpit Bible or make a cardboard replica of a Bible and place it on a Bible stand in front of the speaker's seat. A real sword or fencer's lance laid across it is effective, but one made of foil-clad cardboard works as well. "Word of God" is the blue-ribboned message for this one.

Menu

For a hearty banquet, serve roast beef and all the trimmings or, for more modest budgets, feature Sloppy Joes.

Program

Invite a local coach to be the guest speaker for this occasion or check with your church friends to see who could give a martial arts demonstration. If you're in the mood for films, rent a humorous or inspirational sports video.

A more informal father-son occasion could feature an arm wrestling contest.

Devotions

Your devotion will naturally center around Ephesians 6. Other ideas for devotional talks include stories of the early gladiators, the crowns of Scripture (see II Timothy 4:8, James 1:12, and Revelation 2:10, or I Corinthians 9:24-27).

Sensational
Occasions

Mystery

MYSTERY DINNER

Mystery dinners are great fun for all ages and can be adapted for almost any occasion. They especially lend themselves to appreciation parties planned and served by teens for their teachers, parents, church officers, and so on.

The basic idea is simple. Each guest is given a pre-printed menu and told to order from it. Guests are not told that they must also order all eating utensils. Waiters are not allowed to help explain the menu, on which all foods and eating utensils are cleverly disguised. This is the time to be merciless—what the customer orders is what the customer gets!

The hilarity starts when a guest attempts to eat gelatin with a toothpick, spaghetti with bare fingers, or peas with nothing but a knife. Napkins, too, must be ordered, and many an unwary participant has wound up with egg on the face and goo on the fingers!

Decorations

These can be as simple or as elaborate as you care to make them. Since the mystery dinner is adaptable to any season or holiday, use whatever the occasion calls for. Generally, however, since this is a dinner served in courses, if your tables can be arranged in a cozy restaurant fashion, it will work best. Adding a folding card table here and there among your usual banquet tables will help set the atmosphere of intimate dining.

One teen group once served the adults at a Valentine's Day Sweetheart Banquet, so table decorations consisted of hearts, flowers, and valentines. Bowls of candy hearts, jelly beans, and "message" hearts were set on the tables as emergency rations for those who failed to order properly.

The teens transformed the fellowship hall into the *Café el Torrido*, "the place for red hot lovers!" Teen waiters and waitresses wore formal evening clothes. This elegant cafe even boasted a hatcheck girl (a football player disguised in a blonde wig, short skirt, and so on).

Menu

A number of appetizers, several entrees, a couple of vegetable choices, various breads, drinks, and desserts give the menu variety. The more complicated you make the menu, the less likely anyone is to succeed in ordering correctly.

Our teens created their printed valentine menus out of white construction paper adorned with red hearts and doilies. The bill of fare looked like the following, *minus* the explanations enclosed in parentheses:

Primum Coursum (First Course)

Sweethearts' Gelée (strawberry gelatin)
Lovers' Speciala (green onion stuck through Lifesaver candy)
Bunny's Delite (carrot sticks)
Grenario Circumvenio (tossed green salad)
Strictly Kosher (kosher dill pickle)
Celeree à la Carter (celery stuffed with peanut butter)

Argentum Necessitum (Utensils)

Tyned Speerie (fork)
El Spreadero (knife)
Los Blottero (napkin)
El Shovela (spoon)
El Spearo (toothpick)

Venter Stoffers (Stomach Stuffers, or main course)

Mama Mia à la Romeo (lasagna or spaghetti)
El Spéciala Hombre Destituto (pork and beans)

A la Bakerie (Bakery)

Pain Bis or Pain Maize (French bread or corn bread)

Borracho's Bibcre (Drinker's Corner)

Punch Passionata (red punch)
Espresso (coffee)
Darjeeling thé (tea)
Timbre Floata (toothpick in glass of water)

Never Do This to Your Valentine (Dessert)

Ooo la la Cheesecake (As a joke, serve a catalog bathing suit model's picture—of the appropriate sex—on a dessert plate before actually serving cherry cheesecake.)
Whipped Washington Jubilee (Cherries Jubilee)

(Note: Order at your own risk! Guests who try to intimidate the waiters into ordering for them will be cheerfully banished!)

Program

Serving the food and watching the antics will take up most of the evening, so not much of a program is required. However, to add a little spice to the evening, you can hold a mystery auction.

Hide silly items—such as a bent nail, tissue, a corncob, one earring, a pack of gum—in small lunch bags. The auctioneer pantomimes what's in the bag and then begins auctioning it off. Use play money or, if this is a fund-raising event, hard cash. Much of the success of the auction depends on the comic skills of the auctioneer.

For a sweetheart banquet, couples can be given a margarine tub full of water, which the women must feed to their dates spoonful by spoonful. The first couple to finish wins a silly prize. Other couple games could include the Lifesaver-on-a-toothpick relay (Each team member must place a toothpick in his or her mouth. With hands behind their backs and standing in a line, they pass a Lifesaver candy down the line using only the toothpicks. The first team to finish wins.) or a mummy wrap (Each woman is given a roll of toilet tissue, which she must wrap around her date, mummy-fashion. Again, the first couple to finish wins.).

Variations

For a simplified variation, serve a normal menu. The mystery is in the eating utensils. As guests come in the door, they must reach into a huge grab bag. What they pull out is their only eating utensil for the entire evening. Of course, they are not told this until dinner is served! Fill the grab bag with all sorts of items: egg beater, toy shovel, wooden spoon, toothpick, chopstick (one!), spatula, measuring cup, ice cream scoop, and so forth.

Another simplified variation is a Sunday Surprise. Disguise all the sundae fixings, as well as the eating utensils. Again, guests order at their own risk—and may spend the evening eating only chocolate topping with a straw!

Devotions

Center your devotions around I Corinthians 13, the love chapter; John 3:16, God's great love for us; or the "mysteries" of Scripture, such as the wisdom of God (I Corinthians 2:7), or the Resurrection (I Corinthians 15:51), or the marriage of Christ to the church (Ephesians 5:32).

Symphony

LIFE IS A SYMPHONY

Psalm 150 declares, "Praise God in his sanctuary.
. . . Praise him with the sounding of the trumpet, praise him
with the harp and lyre . . . praise him with the strings and
flute, praise him with the clash of cymbals" (1, 3-5 NIV).

A musical evening can strike a new note for church potlucks.
Choir parties, visiting college choirs, a church musical evening, recognition of school band or chorus members, the
installation of a new minister of music—all are occasions to pull
out the stops and let the music soar.

Decorations

For table decorations, form large musical notes from folded cardboard, so that they will stand independently. Lay fresh or silk flowers
at the base to add color. Black strips of crêpe paper and more notes
make an attractive musical staff backdrop behind the speaker's table.
For your centerpiece, arrange small musical instruments, such as
flutes, violins, or even pieces from a Sunday school rhythm band.

Program and Menu

Compose the printed program to resemble an authentic
symphony program. It will be a highlight of this dinner. The

cover should carry the title, "Life Is a Symphony." It can be embellished with line drawings of several instruments. Make this cover as attractive and professional-looking as possible.

Arrange to have Psalm 150:1-6 printed on page 1, as well as the theme song, Beatrice Bush Bixler's chorus, "Life Is a Symphony."

Skip to page 4 to print the title, "Production Efforts," and to list the banquet committee, under the headings "Arranger/ Director," "Stage and Set Direction," and "Concessions."

In the centerfold, print the menu, written to resemble that on the next page.

SYMPHONY IN E-A-T
(Hungarian Rhapsody)
by the Entire Company

McDonald's Farm
(Ham)

What Did Idaho?
(Baked Potatoes)

Moonlight Sonata
(Assorted Salads)

The Bunny Hop
(Buttered Carrots)

Shortnin' Bread
(Biscuits)

Everything Is Beautiful
(Apple Pie à la mode)

Tea for Two
(Beverages)

The actual program is outlined below.

COMMAND PERFORMANCE

LIFE IS A SYMPHONY

Part I

Overture.. Conductor (name)
Praylude... Invocation

Part II

Tummy Tuneup (Dinner)

Part III

Fun Fanfare...................................... Group Singing

Part IV

Spiritual Dynamics.......................................Speaker
"In Tune with Christ"

Grand Finale
"Life is a Symphony"
(Curtain)

If you have the budget, the remainder of the program booklet could contain the words to the songs used in the fun fanfare. Your choice of songs depends on the occasion for the dinner. Be sure to check copyrights before copying song lyrics. Use only those that are in public domain. Or, if your church subscribes to a copyright service, use those for which you have permission.

Progressive Dinner

PILGRIM'S PROGRESS

John Bunyan's famous classic, *Pilgrim's Progress*, lends itself beautifully as a theme for a progressive dinner. Most of the courses will be served in individual homes (see "Program" for locations), so this works best with a small group, like a Sunday school class. It can be easily adapted for any age group, but a children's party would have to have adult drivers. A women's group may want to adapt it to a tour of several homes or gardens.

To use the theme for a larger group, skip the progressive dinner and serve the meal as a banquet in the church fellowship hall. Set the mood for each separate course by reading a few paragraphs describing Christian's stops along the way.

Decorations

Host families will want to decorate their serving areas to represent their assigned places. When the entire dinner is served in one place, decorate with anything mentioned in the book having to do with Christian's climb Heavenward, or use simple American pilgrim decorations—turkeys, pilgrim hats, dried corn, Plymouth Rock, or the Mayflower.

113

Directions to participating homes, printed on programs, will lead your guests to the correct addresses. Design the programs like miniature pilgrim hats.

Menu

Serve the meal in courses, beginning with appetizers at the first stop. These can be anything the host family wishes to serve.

Serve soup, preferably clam chowder, at the second residence; salad at the third home. The main meal, consisting of turkey, dressing, whipped potatoes, and kernel corn, will require a larger dining area. You may want to schedule this stop for "the Palace Beautiful," the church fellowship hall.

Weather permitting, serve beverages at a serene river or lakeside, to represent the "River of Life," where Christian was greatly refreshed on his journey. This would be a good place to stop for recreation.

A light dessert course, perhaps a gelatin salad, can be served in the "Delectable Mountains of Immanuel's Land" (if one of your host families lives on a hill!).

Postpone the final course, coffee and pumpkin pie, until after the program. It can be served in the same location in which the program is held, or the group can move on to a final stop, possibly the pastor's or Sunday school teacher's home.

Program

Christian stopped at many places on his journey but did not eat at some of them. Purists will want to make certain they assign to host families only those locations at which food actually was served in the story. For instance, at the "Palace Beautiful," Christian was given bread, drink, and a cluster of raisins to help him through the "Valley of Humiliation." He was refreshed with food and drink at the "River of Life," in the

"Delectable Mountains," and, of course, at the "Marriage Supper" in the "Celestial City."

Host homes could also portray the "House of the Interpreter," "Vanity Fair," the "Slough of Despond," or "Bypath Meadow." At each home, the host and hostess should wear signs with the names of the characters they represent. At the "House of the Interpreter," for example, the Interpreter is the host, assisted by his sons, Passion and Patience. Watchful is the porter at the "Palace Beautiful"; The Shepherds—Knowledge, Experience, Watchful, and Sincere—guide Christian through the "Delectable Mountains."

At each home, after that portion of the meal is served, the host or hostess can read the passage from *Pilgrim's Progress* that deals with that location. Condense the reading to involve only a page or two at the most.

Feature the popular colonial game of "Stool Ball" for recreation at the "River of Life." The participants sit on stools, arranged in a large circle, or flat stones. The person who is "it" throws a ball into the air. Every player must change positions, running from one stool to another. "It" tries to recover the ball and throw it at a player before he or she reaches a stool. If "it" is successful, the tagged player becomes "it"; otherwise, the original leader tries again. Because of the agility it takes to get up and run from such a low position, this game furnishes loads of laughs.

Christian's obstacle course also makes a hilarious event. Divide into teams and run the obstacle course relay-fashion. Obstacles could include the "Slough of Despond" (walking across a shallow pool of water on rocks or a log), climbing the "Hill of Difficulty" (walking up a playground slide), going through the "Valley of the Shadow" (crawling under a blanket-draped picnic table), navigating the "Valley of Humiliation" (continuing on hands and knees through a series of old tires), and finally, making it through the "Wicket Gate" (a large cardboard box with open ends).

115

If the party is held in one place, you may want to try some paper and pencil games. Scramble the names of places in the book and set a time limit for unscrambling, or pin the name of a character from the book on the back of each person. All must try to determine one another's identity by asking questions that can be answered only with a yes or a no.

Your Christian film supplier no doubt has the classic "Pilgrim's Progress" in the film version, or its sequel, "Christiana." Either of these would make an excellent program selection. Churches with lower budgets may want to use the flashcard story available from Bible Visuals, Inc., Box 93, Landisville, Pennsylvania 17538.

Variations

For a different kind of party, try a fast-food progressive dinner. The group begins by eating onion rings or French fries for appetizers at one fast-food restaurant. Then the group goes to another place for hamburgers or pizza, to an ice cream parlor for dessert, and back to the host's home for espresso.

An "Around the World" theme also works well for progressive dinners. Each host family serves a dish from a foreign country and decorates with items from that country.

Hillbilly

HILLBILLY HOEDOWN

There's nothing like a foot-stompin', toe-tappin' hoedown to make people let down their hair, break through the barriers of stuffed-shirtitis, and really get to know their neighbors. A hillbilly hoedown is a fun-filled dinner suitable for any casual occasion, for any age group.

Because it's reminiscent of the old-time barn raisings or dinners-on-the-grounds so popular in rural America years ago, senior-citizen groups will especially enjoy this one. A hoedown is also a good choice for groups that want a Halloween costume party without the ghouls, witches, and ghosts.

Decorations

Take a cue from TV's "Hee Haw" for decorations and costumes. Ears of corn, bales of straw, plank and sawhorse tables, checkered tablecloths, scarecrows—let your imagination run free.

Costumes of bright bandanas, straw hats, bib overalls, cut-off jeans, plaid shirts, and extravagant neckties are easy, inexpensive, and fun to make and wear.

Check out Salvation Army or Good Will stores for old hats. Embellish them with flowers and feathers and use for clever centerpieces. Don't forget to dangle the pricetags for these perky "Minnie Pearl" creations!

Menu

No fancy stuff here! Just plain ole down-home cookin'. Fried chicken is a must, served with buttermilk biscuits, mashed potatoes (or yams or potato salad), okra, black-eyed peas, corn bread, grits, and plenty of greens. Mayonnaise cake or pecan pie will finish stuffing the tummies.

Old Fashioned Fried Chicken

8 to 10 roasting chickens (about 40 lbs.)
1 qt. buttermilk

Coating:
2 lbs. sifted flour
5 tbsp. salt
1 tbsp. each, black pepper, garlic powder, onion powder, paprika
1 tsp. ground sage, ground thyme
1/2 tsp. baking powder

Cut chicken into serving pieces. Wash and pat dry; place in large flat dish. Pour buttermilk over chicken; cover and let soak for at least 1 hour or overnight in refrigerator. Combine coating ingredients in double strength paper bag and shake chicken pieces, a few at a time, to coat well. Lay coated pieces on waxed paper for about 15 minutes to allow coating to dry (this will help coating cling better during frying).

Saute chicken pieces until golden brown on both sides in hot shortening in heavy skillets (about 3 minutes per side). Reduce heat and simmer chicken, turning occasionally, for 25–35 minutes or until chicken is tender. Drain on paper towels and serve. Makes 50 servings.

Program

The program can be as simple as a "Gospel singing"—lots of rousing, toe-tapping choruses and Stamps-Baxter style hymns. Camp-meetin' music, such as "I'll Fly Away," "Victory in Jesus," "That Old Time Religion," "Living By Faith," and "Camping in Canaan's Land" will delight any group. Music will, of course, be accompanied by guitars and fiddles.

A longer affair could include a pie-eating contest, a hat-judging contest for the zaniest hat, a log-roll (using fireplace logs), or a tractor pull (use large tricycles for the tractors).

For a youth group activity, you'll have great fun with a Sadie Hawkin's Day race, where the gals go after the guys of their choice. Guys get a five-minute head start to hide. The first girl to drag her "catch" in is the bride for a silly, mock hillbilly wedding. Guests use their imaginations to deck the honoree in proper weddin' clothes (using a tablecloth, curtains, or whatever is handy).

"Marryin' Sam" will then perform the wedding, using something ridiculous, like the following, for the "wedding vows," all in a hillbilly dialect.

"Friends, revenuers, fellow hillbillies, lend me your ears and your shotguns. We've come to marry _____, not to bury him!

"Dearly beloved, we'uns is gathered heah on this happy occasion to yew-nite this heah man and this heah woman in the honerable state of matrimony. We all knows marriage is a honerable institution, but who wants to spend his life in a institution?

"As I was sayin', nobudy should oughter enter into it unless he cain't get out of it nohow. Whoops, I mean nobudy should enter into it lightly or without giving it lots of thinkin'.

"Notice this purty white gown the bride heah is awearin'?

119

White is sposed to be the symbol of purity and happiness. Now, didja ever wonder why the groom is awearin' black?

"And yal knows how they give a shower fer the bride and not fer the groom? That's cause the groom ain't aneedin' any showers—he's all washed up anyhow!

"Wal, if any of yal knows any reason whatsoever why this heah man and woman cain't be lawfully jerned tergether, speak up right now or ferever shut up.

"Young man, will ya take this heah woman to be yer lawful wedded wife? Will ya love her and honer her and keep her barefoot the rest of her life?

"And young woman, will ya take this heah fine gentleman to be yer wedded husband? Will ya obey him, keep his socks darned, fetch his slippers, and keep lots of vittles on his table?

"Now, who has the ball and chain—I mean the ring fer this young man's nose—er, his finger? This heah ring is a token of the fact that yew was caught good and proper, and that from this day ferward, yew is considered uneligible to participate in any more Sadie Hawkin's Day Races."

Devotions

The Bible has a lot to say about hills and mountains. Use Psalm 121:1, "I lift up my eyes to the hills," or Matthew 5:14, "A city on a hill cannot be hidden," to spark your devotional thoughts.

Hobo Party

HOBO HILARITY

Almost everyone enjoys "dressing down," so this hobo theme can be used at just about any time. Try it for a farewell dinner, a youth group event, a family fun frolic, a Halloween party, a father-son outing, or a Scout activity.

Decorations

Since atmosphere is important, the hobo theme works best around a campfire at an abandoned shanty, shack, or barn. Second best, but still effective, is a recreation room-turned-hobo-heaven.

To transform an indoor area into a hobo retreat, make a phony campfire with electric or gas logs. Paper or wood railroad tracks, a "stop-look-listen" sign, and old railroad lanterns would also help create your hobo "yards."

Tables are wooden planks laid across sawhorses and spread with newspapers. Decorate your tables with colorful bandana bundles tied to the ends of sticks.

Guests should come dressed in their hobo best, with a prize awarded for the funniest outfit. First prize? What else but a can of pork and beans and a cheap can opener! The costumes will add to your decorations, not to mention the free-wheeling hilarity of the guests.

Menu

Each guest will bring eating utensils—aluminum pie plates or tin cans, plus a tin cup or fruit jar for beverages. Therefore, the menu must be a simple, one-course dish. Use your favorite stew recipe and call it "Ramblin' Stew" or "Hobo Hash." Serve it with biscuits and plenty of hot coffee (preferably brewed over the open fire). Doughnuts, roasted marshmallows, or a "snatched watermelon" will be sufficient for dessert. The proverbial pork and beans from a can is another good menu choice.

If this is a campfire supper, hobo packets make a simple, yet delicious, meal. Double-wrap a sliced raw potato, an onion, and a carrot with a hamburger patty in aluminum foil for each person. Cook over hot coals for about 45 minutes or until done.

Open-fire orange biscuits bake up a hearty accompaniment. Cut oranges in half. Scoop out the fruit and save for dessert. Fill the half-orange shells with prepared biscuit mix and place them in warm coals until the biscuits are baked. The "baking pans" give a scrumptious orange flavor to the dough. The beauty of this menu is that there are no dishes to wash, since the "cookware" also doubles as the serving dish and can be thrown away.

Program

Fireside skits, tales of famous hobos, and hobo tall tales make for impromptu fun. Of course, you must include the hobo shuffle (the parade of hobos for costume judging).

A frog jumping contest could be a really special attraction. Each team catches its own frog. A large circle is drawn in the dirt, and the frogs are placed in the middle. The first frog to escape the circle wins!

Whether true or not, legend has it that hobos snatch watermelons. Design a treasure hunt routed around the area, with a juicy watermelon as the treasure. The first team to locate it gets first dibs on the melon.

Devotions

Hobos like to call themselves "Knights of the Road" or "Happy Wanderers." Devotions based on the wandering prodigal son (Luke 15:11-32) or the wanderings of the Israelites in the wilderness (Exodus) make an effective message.

Tea Party

DOLLY AND ME TEA PARTY

What little girl—or big girl, for that matter—hasn't dreamed of dressing in lace and frills to attend a tea party in the spirit of Alice in Wonderland?

A tea party works well as an opener or social for mothers of the nursery or cradle roll. It can also serve as a mother and daughter banquet, or it can be held to honor female graduates and their mothers and grandmothers or to welcome youngsters being promoted from the beginning ranks to the primary grades. It could also set the theme for a baby shower.

Decorations

Raid the play room for dolls, dollhouses, and toy tea sets to use as centerpieces and decorations grouped together in displays. You can go with a hodgepodge of dolls or specify antique dolls, homemade dolls, rag dolls, Barbie dolls, bride dolls, or paper dolls. If the party is for youngsters, encourage them to bring their favorite doll buddy for a "Kid and Me Dinner."

Use lacy tablecloths and china, if available, to create an elegant, storybook charm.

Menu

Serve delectable finger sandwiches, miniature tarts, petit fours, lady fingers, éclairs, scones and honey, nuts, and mints in your prettiest serving dishes. Offer a variety of herbal or spiced teas for beverage.

Program

If this potluck is used in conjunction with an open house or promotion of youngsters from one class to another, the department superintendent or teachers can explain the purpose and goals of the nursery or cradle roll. Plan the program to show off what the youngsters have learned in the class.

An older group, such as a mother-daughter affair, would enjoy "How to Be a Real Doll," a demonstration by a beauty or fashion consultant. A finishing-school instructor is another possible guest speaker. Or how about a shape-up pep talk by an aerobics leader, dance instructor, or other fitness expert?

Devotions

Center Scripture readings around the image of God, the beauty of Jesus, or a talk on inner beauty.

Variations

Have a toy party, using any group or variety of toys as your centerpieces and decorations. Serve grilled cheese or peanut butter and honey sandwiches with a variety of chips and dips. Decorate a cake to look like Raggedy Ann, a teddy bear, or a toy train—whatever fits your theme. The kids will be grateful that you went to so much trouble for them. Even small children like creative programs!

Gypsy Party

GYPSY RENDEZVOUS

There's nothing like romantic music and the warm glow of a campfire under a star-studded sky to put people in a thoughtful mood. A gypsy rendezvous works best when it is held out under the stars, preferably in a grove, an orchard, or a barnyard. But it also can work in a church fellowship hall as a sweethearts' banquet, a youth group gathering, or as a total church fellowship.

Use in-church musicians dressed in gypsy attire to set the mood with haunting gypsy melodies, such as "My Little Gypsy Sweetheart." If you can, persuade everyone to dress as gypsies.

Decorations

An outside party won't require many decorations. Simply arrange the area like a gypsy camp. Inside you may want to set the mood with cloth-covered hay bales, old wagon wheels, and brightly colored shawls draped along the walls.

Empty pop bottles used as vases for wildflowers carry out the vagabond theme as centerpieces. Burlap squares in the middle of each table are all the table covering you will need.

Menu

Serve fondue, asking everyone to bring fondue pots. Or improvise, using pierced tin cans set over candles to hold your chafing dishes.

Cube angel food cake and sweet breads. Cut up fresh fruits such as apples, bananas, pineapple, strawberries, and oranges. Provide a choice of chocolate or vanilla sauce for dipping.

For a fun meal, use meatballs or chunks of roast beef and tater tots to be dipped in hot oil. Provide a cheese sauce for dipping fresh veggies.

Or try Hungarian goulash for a completely different menu choice. Here's one excellent recipe for it:

Hearty Hungarian Goulash

1 tbsp. oil	2 tbsp. flour
1½ lbs. beef cubes	1 cup water
1 envelope onion-mushroom	8 oz. broad egg noodles
soup mix	salt to taste
1½ tbsp. paprika	
16 oz. can stewed tomatoes	

In a large saucepan, heat the oil and brown the beef. Add the soup mix and paprika blended with tomatoes. Simmer covered, stirring occasionally, 1½ hours until beef is tender. Stir in flour and salt blended with water. Bring to a boil; then simmer, stirring constantly, until sauce is thickened, about 5 minutes. Meanwhile, cook the noodles according to package directions. Serve the goulash over the noodles. Serves 6.

Program

Have a scavenger hunt, listing specific items to be brought back. The first team to return with the most items wins. Or give the teams instructions to bring back the most unusual thing they can find in a specified time limit. If you're in the country, you'll never know what you might find—you might see the teams bring back a menagerie of horses, cows, or chickens. Just make sure everything is returned to its owner!

A thieves' market trade-up is a great variation of the scavenger hunt. Give each team an object of little value—a penny, a banana, a paper clip, or a pencil. Teams must invade the community to trade their objects for something of increased value. They continue trading upward until they feel they have transacted their best deal in the allotted time. The winning team is the one whose "treasure" has the greatest monetary value. The objects can then be auctioned off or donated to charity.

Groups in rural and small towns should have no trouble with these activities. But those in urban or metropolitan areas may want to stick to homes of church members, neighbors, or friends.

A campfire sing-along is a pleasant way to end the evening. One song that would fit very well is "Just a Wayfaring Stranger."

Devotions

Scripture readings and a devotional message could center around Christians being a unique group of people, set apart from the world. A good reading would be Ephesians 2:19.

Mexican Fiesta

OLÉ!

With the hispanic population fast becoming the number one ethnic group in the United States, churches need to assess their ministries to this growing community. Have a Mexican fiesta as an opportunity to share with a Spanish congregation in your community or as a planning time to evaluate your outreach to the area's hispanics. "Olé" is also an effective theme when you are entertaining missionaries from Mexico or any South or Central American country, or for youth group occasions. Kids love Mexican food!

Other events to celebrate with this idea are Cinco de Mayo (May 5) and dies y seis de Septiembre (September 16). Both are big patriotic holidays in Mexico.

Decorations

Colorful is the key word for tablecloths and accessories. Drape Mexican ponchos and serapes along the walls, interspersed with an occasional sombrero. South of the border souvenirs, potted cacti, bright tissue paper flowers as centerpieces and displays will make everyone say, "Olé!" Where possible, group small tables in intimate settings with candles set in old bottles on each table. Add several enormous paper flowers to complete your bright fiesta.

Hang a piñata, to be broken by the children during the program. For a very special touch, why not put together a strolling mariachi band to play its romantic music during the meal, using Spanish guitar, accordion, maracas, and tambourine.

Menu

Serve tacos salad bar style, allowing everyone to add his or her own seasonings. Inventive cooks are always creating new possibilities for taco makings. Standard taco fare includes flour or corn tortillas, hamburger, shredded chicken or beef, refried beans, chopped onions, tomatoes, lettuce, peppers, black olives, shredded cheeses, and a variety of toppings, such as guacamole, sour cream, and several intensities of salsa.

On each table, place baskets of tortilla chips with a bowl of salsa for appetizers. For dessert, serve *sopiapillas* (a type of Mexican scone) with honey, *crustos*, or an array of Mexican sweet breads or exotic fresh fruits.

Program

A sing-along of Spanish hymns and choruses will provide lots of fun as the "anglos" attempt to pronounce the foreign words in time to familiar melodies. Use an overhead projector to write phonetically the words from a Spanish hymnal. Show a Spanish language film; Moody Films, 820 N. LaSalle Street, Chicago, Illinois 60610, has a good supply available, or check with your local film distributor. Watching a movie in another language is a good experience because you learn what it feels like to be constantly surrounded by a foreign tongue.

Rio Grande Bible College, 4300 S. Business 281, Edinburgh, Texas 78539, trains hispanic nationals to return to their countries to preach the gospel. Perhaps you could have a presentation or some literature from them as part of your program. If a missionary to Mexico or a South or Central American country is in your area, by all means, ask that person to speak. If you have invited a Spanish congregation to join you, ask the Spanish pastor to share with your group.

For a current events program, have a panel discussion on the church's role in giving sanctuary to illegal aliens, providing citizenship or English-as-a-second-language classes, ministering to migrant workers, or easing tensions between hispanic and anglo factions in the community.

For a fun event, have a demonstration on how to make a piñata from balloons, papier mâché, and crêpe paper.

Devotions

The tone of your program will dictate what devotions you will have, if any. If you're featuring a missionary or a hispanic pastor, give him or her leeway in choosing devotional passages. If devotions follow a discussion of illegal aliens or inauguration of or graduation from a citizenship class, use the devotions to reflect on what being a citizen of God's kingdom means. Romans 8:2 reminds us that the law of the Spirit of life in Jesus has made us free from the law of sin and death. I Corinthians 7:22-23 reminds us of what it cost for God to buy our citizenship.

Scripture passages reminding Christians of their responsibility to their fellow inhabitants on this earth could wind up a discussion on helping migrants or healing community distrust and tension. Passages such as Matthew 5:39-48 and Luke 6:27-38 are humbling reminders that there is no place for selfishness and discord in the lives of believers.

Oriental Feast

ORIENTAL GARDEN

Bring a taste of the Orient to your next church fellowship by creating the aura of an Oriental garden or restaurant. This idea works well for any group that enjoys ethnic food or likes to try something different.

Decorations

Set the mood with Oriental screens, Japanese lanterns, origami, fans, giant paper flowers, and miniature Bonsai trees. Have your resident artist copy Japanese or Chinese symbols down the middle of newsprint for a nifty tablecloth. Print the symbols on plain paper napkins, plates, and cups for matching accessories.

To add some humor to the meal, test everyone's dexterity by placing chopsticks at each place instead of silverware. Have silverware available after the first five minutes or so!

Menu

Serve chow mein or beef and walnut Cantonese, accompanied by fried rice. Or set up a wok at each table and stir fry the meal while the hungry guests watch. For a beverage, provide a variety of Oriental teas. Finish the meal with fortune cookies. For a unique touch, make your own fortune cookies with prophetic verses or Bible promises placed inside.

Program

Rig a ceremonial gong to announce each phase of the meal and program. Printed programs should be imprinted with a silhouette of a Bonsai tree or other Oriental symbols. Each section can be introduced with a "Confucious-like" saying.

The type of program is determined by the purpose of the gathering. Have an informative seminar on the religions of the Orient or invite an Oriental exchange student or missionary to share personal experiences with your group. Slides of the Orient could be set to Oriental music. Or have a martial arts demonstration, a Japanese cooking demonstration, or a how-to on Japanese flower arranging or origami.

Devotions

For a missions-oriented gathering, show a film on Hudson Taylor or tell the story of other missionaries to the Orient. Read some of the Bible's wisdom literature, such as Proverbs, to see how it compares with wise Oriental sayings.

Patterns

PATTERNS FOR LIVING

This program is designed for any of those "Women's Nights Out" on your annual agenda. It is ideal for mother-daughter banquets, graduation teas, installation dinners for women's circles, or women's meetings at denominational conventions.

Decorations

Cover tables with fabric remnants or white newsprint to which dress pattern pieces have been attached. Sewing tools or notions—zippers, thread, buttons, scissors, measuring tapes—are made-to-fit centerpiece arrangements. The centerpiece for the head table could be a large sewing basket full of flowers, a tailor's dress form surrounded with notions, or even a portable sewing machine artfully decorated with fabric and flowers.

If you want, give party favors of small baby-food jars whose lids have been padded and covered with calico and then tied with bright ribbon. The jars can later serve as pincushions and button holders.

Set a real pattern envelope at each place to serve as a program holder. Numbered pattern pieces drawn on plain paper contain the segments of the program. Or draw small pattern pieces on a single sheet and type in the program parts (see sketch). A display

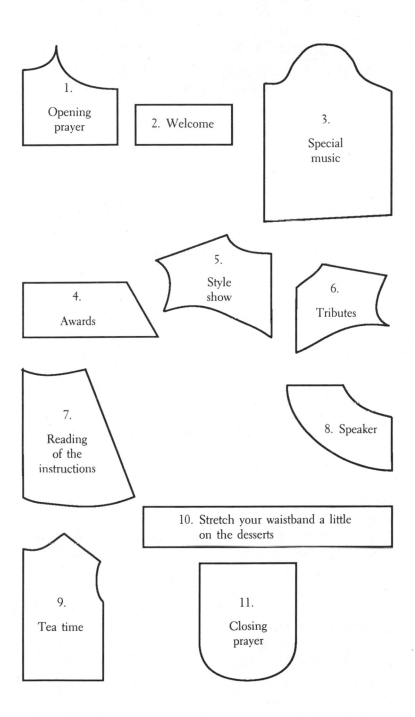

1. Opening prayer

2. Welcome

3. Special music

4. Awards

5. Style show

6. Tributes

7. Reading of the instructions

8. Speaker

9. Tea time

10. Stretch your waistband a little on the desserts

11. Closing prayer

of dated pattern envelopes and ancient sewing tools and machines could produce a lot of laughs.

Menu

Since many women in today's diet-conscious world are watching their weight, this is a good time for a salad bar. Huge dishpans full of lettuce surrounded by an assortment of vegetables and garnishes make for easy serving. For large crowds, you may want to have several salad bars set up. Planted sign-post fashion in each bowl of lettuce, this little ditty says it all:

> Hey, diddle diddle,
> I'm watching my middle.
> I'm hoping to slim it quite soon.
> But eating's such fun,
> I won't get it done
> Till my dish runs away with my spoon!

An elegant low-calorie dessert would be in keeping with this menu. You might want to "reward" the group for their calorie-consciousness with something a little more fattening— strawberry tarts and low-cal dessert topping, a single-crust pie, or a cart of assorted moderate-calorie desserts.

Program

A fashion show would fit with the patterns theme. Display mother-daughter fashions, bridal gowns (a fun way to show off those old gowns that still fit!), or "styles of yesteryear" (raid those old trunks in the attic).

For an absolutely hilarious time, you might want to try something like the following, which a denominational group in Illinois did for its annual women's tea. The outfits were suited to the descriptions.

136

Fashions of the Heart

Fashion Narrator: Fresh from the social circles of London, Tessie True Brew is wearing her tea-party dress. The lines for this basic shift are flowing, so there is no strain. Notice that the waist is cinched by a novelty belt that's just right for the occasion. This dress comes in three blends, orange, black, and green pekoe. Tiny spaghetti straps add just a touch of Italian flavor to the dress. Tessie has accessorized this outfit with a perfect little hat and box purse. So, ladies, if you need a little dress to wear to all those summer teas coming up, this may be just your bag. Unfortunately, this dress is not washable or dry cleanable—but dip it in boiling water, make two dozen sandwiches, and invite sixteen friends for a party that's out of this world!

(Outfit—Long nightgown, covered with beige pillowcases, stuffed like teabags. Belt has cups tied to it; cups dangle from string for earrings. Actual tea bags are pinned on the dress; real spaghetti is fastened to straps of nightgown. Wear tea strainer as hat. Carry a large tea box for purse.)

Narrator: Bertha Bachsholder (Boxholder) is modeling a lovely Kellogg's original, a woman-tailored three-piece box suit. The tie belt at the waist is color-coordinated with the darling blouse. Notice the green frog closing at the neckline. This box suit is made from the famous Kantwet fiberboard. It is guaranteed not to wrinkle (if you can sit down), and is easy to pack for traveling—just fold flat. The pillbox hat gives the ensemble the finished look. After wearing this creation all day, you will need the pills on the hat!

(Outfit—Large Kellogg's cereal packing box, with holes cut out for arms and neck. Frilly, long-sleeved blouse, with plastic green frog prominently displayed at neckline. A child's stuffed frog or Muppet hand puppet slung around neck will work equally well. A small packing box for aspirin tied to head with a large bow serves as the pillbox.)

Narrator: Sally Sweet Tooth is here, fresh from the Sears catalog. She is wearing a Brach's original ensemble. The skirt is crisply fashioned of Sears sucker, in a geometric print that is paper thin. Made for easy care, this fabric features no wash, no iron—just give it a lick and a promise. This sweet little skirt, teamed with a raglan sleeve blouse, is always in good taste.

(Outfit—Skirt made of geometric print wrapping paper, covered with rows of candy suckers. Blouse with ragged sleeves. Model licks on a giant candy sucker.)

Narrator: This lovely ensemble, worn by Dottie Dash, is great for the lady who is always on the go. This cancan skirt is very easy to care for. The material is light and comfortable, perfect for those hot summer days. And when she gets tired of this outfit, she can recycle it.

You may have heard the saying, "The 'hurrier' I go, the behinder I get." Well, in these smart looking shoes, you'll say, "The 'hurrier' I go, the farther I get."

Notice the charming five-quart headpiece, which Dottie has chosen instead of the normal ten-gallon hat. This hat is extremely handy when she goes to the grocery for a few items.

(Outfit—A row of tin cans dangles from the bottom of a flounced skirt; the model wears roller skates for shoes and a plastic water bucket for a hat.)

Narrator: Harriet Homemaker models this captivating casual house dress, designed by the House of Fabrics in a richly textured polished cotton. The fabric is strong and durable. Notice the intricate construction details. The charming belt is the perfect fashion accessory and coordinates splendidly with the hat.

(Outfit—Simple shift dress covered with construction paper houses. Model wears a carpenter's nail apron, complete with hammer, pliers, tape measure, and other tools, and carries a roll of construction blueprints. She wears a bright yellow hard hat to complete the ensemble.)

Narrator: Sleep-City Sue models an after-five dinner gown, so right for your evening engagements. Accented by a bow at the back, the gown is trimmed in lace with a ruffle at the bottom. Very attractive, yet comfortable, the gown is accented with plush evening slippers. The white knit turban completes this lovely evening wear ensemble.

(Outfit—Flannel nightgown, fuzzy slippers, and silly night hat.)

Narrator: Ladies, you will love to tiptoe through the tulips in this tulip red marshmallow crêpe dress. It is a lovely outfit for a garden party or for a marshmallow roast. Tootsie Tulip's tiny waist is accentuated by a beautiful soft white sash, which coordinates perfectly with the new marshmallow necklace. You will not want to miss this tasteful buy—you'll look just yummy in it!

(Outfit—Red crêpe paper dress, strung marshmallows for sash and necklace. Huge paper tulip worn in hair.)

Narrator: Betsy Businesswoman wears a conservative pantdress that declares she has arrived. Designed for the successful executive who likes to show her colors, this red, white, and blue ensemble will be the talk of the office. This tricky little number would also be perfect for that Fourth of July picnic; just add a firecracker or two. Accompanying this lovely suit is an appropriate tie belt.

(Outfit—Two pairs of huge navy blue men's pants fastened on the shoulder by the cuffs, jumper fashion. Man's necktie around the middle for a belt. Red, white, and blue stars attached to the pants. Model carries small American flags, wears flag earrings, and a straw hat.)

Narrator: Miss Ringie-Dingie from Bell Isle presents a very striking tone in these unique bell jeans. She will have music wherever she goes. Completely washable, you just "ring" them dry. To complement the bell jeans, Ringie-Dingie has chosen this bright turtleneck, which holds up very well in water, though it moves slowly. This outfit is designed for the belle of the ball, or would be an excellent choice for a cosmetics saleslady.

(Outfit—Old blue jeans, covered everywhere with tiny jingle bells. White sweater, with rubber turtles attached around neckline. Use construction paper turtles as alternative.)

Narrator: Next we have an elegant bridal gown modeled by Choo-Choo June. June is a vision of loveliness in this creation made of perky percale, imported from the cotton fields back home. This gown is trailed by a clicky little train. The headpiece is held in place by a bobby pin and a lot of hope! The bride carries an Amtrak timetable with a bouquet of dandelions, which add just the right touch for this year's bride on the move.

(Outfit—A child's percale sheet in a train motif and bridal veil pinned on head by a bobby pin. Child's pull-toy train with long string pinned to waist. Organ plays "Bridal Chorus.")

Narrator: Minnie the Maid wears the latest in maid's apparel, designed by Do-It-Yourself, Inc. Notice the stylish high hat, which can be whipped off ever-so-quickly for those last minute dust particles before the guests arrive.

The jewelry is especially helpful during canning season, and the matching purse is not only fashionable but also extremely useful in emergencies. Surely you will agree that this will be a great fashion this season!

(Outfit—Old cleaning dress with household cleaning items attached. Large feather duster on head; necklace and bracelets made of canning rings. Purse is a pail with brushes and cleaning supplies inside.)

Narrator: The high school and college crowd will go ape over this Hedda Hopper Original, a stunning jumpsuit with a plunging neckline. It is especially designed for the sports minded woman. The fabric is a very rare Kangaroo skin, imported from Australia on the slow boat from China.

(Outfit—Any large bag will do—laundry, duffle, or burlap. Model wears a large, colorful bow in her hair and hops down the walkway in the bag.)

Narrator: Vega Bond comes to us from Detroit, wearing the Traveler's Choice car coat. This lovely car coat is lightweight, water repellent, and so neutral that it goes with any outfit. A bit of luxury, yet economically priced. A must for the woman on the go; you can go absolutely anywhere in it.

(Outfit—Large black garbage bag with cut-out armholes and neckline. Glue car pictures all over it. Model carries an umbrella covered with road maps.)

Narrator: Windy Wendy completes our fashion show, wearing a breezy little ensemble full of color. Windy's outfit is especially helpful for those women who are always up in the air about something. It is made from easy-care fabric and is completely washable, though wearing it may present some difficulties. Beware of people bearing pins and stay away from porcupines.

(Outfit—Model is encased in inflated balloons of different shapes, sizes, and colors.)

Devotions

Each pattern jacket should include a *Pattern for Living* instruction sheet, which someone can read at the appropriate time. Instructions are as follows:

Planning the Project: "In all your ways acknowledge him and he will make your paths straight" (Proverbs 3:6 NIV).

Styles: Styles in fashion may change, but the Pattern for Living remains forever the same. "So then, just as you received Christ Jesus as Lord, continue to live in him" (Colossians 2:6 NIV).

Pattern: A design to serve as a model in making something else. "In everything set them an example by doing what is good" (Titus 2:7 NIV).

Measurements: "Grasp how wide and long and high and deep is the love of Christ" (Ephesians 3:18 NIV).

Materials Required: "Love, joy, peace, patience, kindness, goodness, faithfulness, gentleness, and self-control" (Galatians 5:22-23 NIV).

Seam Allowance: Give others the benefit of the doubt. "Man looks at the outward appearance, but the LORD looks at the heart" (I Samuel 16:7 NIV).

Seam: Pieces of material that are joined together. As Christians, "In Christ we who are many form one body, and each member belongs to all the others" (Romans 12:5 NIV).

Ease: When one seamline is longer than the other, fullness is evenly distributed by easing fabric threads together without gathers or puckers. As Christians, we often need to ease things.

"Love is patient, love is kind. It does not envy, it does not boast, it is not proud" (I Corinthians 13:4 NIV).

Pressing: Applying heat and pressure to achieve a smooth, finished garment. "Blessed is the man who perseveres under trial, because when he has stood the test, he will receive the crown of life that God has promised to those who love him" (James 1:12 NIV).

Finishing Details: "I have finished the race, I have kept the faith" (II Timothy 4:7 NIV).

Variations

This idea can be adapted for men's groups or mixed groups by making it "A Blueprint for Living." Use blueprints and builder's tools in place of dress patterns and sewing paraphernalia.

What Next, Charlie Brown?

PEANUTS GANG PIZZA PARTY

Everybody loves Charlie Brown and the Peanuts Gang, and almost everybody loves pizza. Put the two together for instant success. While this theme is adaptable to any age group, it is especially successful with teens. Try it for a youth group graduation bash or for installation of officers.

Decorations

Cover the tables with the comic pages from Sunday newspapers. Graduates' names may be printed on inexpensive plastic dog dishes using permanent paint pens. Use them as centerpieces first and invite guests to add their "John Henrys" and a parting message. Then give them as gifts to your graduates or retiring officers. Construct a "Lucy's Advice Booth" and place it in a conspicuous corner. Peanuts Gang stickers, available at stationery stores, will decorate plain white cups and napkins, or you can splurge on the pre-printed variety.

Transform paper nut cups into dog dishes by gluing or taping a two-inch wide strip of construction paper around the outside. Print a common dog name on the construction paper and fill the bowls with unshelled peanuts. Jars of peanut butter and miniature doghouses made from construction paper are alternative decorations.

Menu

Pizza, and still more pizza! Teens can devour twice their weight in pizza, so be sure to make or order plenty. Offer a variety of toppings for the more particular in your group.

A fun way to serve pizza is to have the crusts and sauce prepared ahead of time and set out on a large table, accompanied by bowls of toppings. Groups of teens together build their own pizzas and then bake and eat them. This works only if you have a small enough group or lots of oven space. Two flour tortillas, with butter in between, make a good crust for individual pizzas.

Peanut-butter cookies and ice-cream cones are the only desserts needed. You can set relish trays on the tables, but don't expect the teens to eat many veggies when there is pizza on hand!

Program

Put construction paper covers on your mimeographed programs and have an artist in your group draw a large picture of Charlie Brown with a "balloon" saying "What Next?" You may want to cut out Peanuts Gang cartoons and paste them to the cover fronts. The kids will have a blast reading one another's covers.

The first page of the program gives the evening's schedule in story form. You could set it up similar to this:

Another Great Story

Once there was this big group of kids, all decked out in their Sunday best, and they were having a party at (name of place). Well, this one guy, a round-faced, bald-headed preacher, got up and asked the blessing on the food.

Then all these famished teens went tearing out to the chow line, where they ate, and ate, and ate, and ate, eatcetera, eatcetera.

After they had devoured everything edible in the joint, the songleader got up and told 'em they'd have to sing for their supper.

Next, the youth-group sponsor said that, seeing as how old officers are like old skiers—they never die, they just go down hill—it was time to install new officers.

At about the same time, the former president declared that it would be a good idea to give out some awards.

Then a "sweet baboo" named (name of soloist) went up front to sing, after which some guy spoke, and spoke, and spoke, and spoke, and spoke, speakcetera, speakcetera.

Finally, another sweet baboo, who got elected as the new president, said it was time to go home, so he [she] prayed the closing prayer. Then he [she] said, "This is the end of the party."

It's also the end of my story.

* * *

For a graduation party, add a class prophecy segment to your program. Write a silly prophecy, using the names and interests of your graduates. Here are a few samples:

Linus Looks Ahead

(A peek at our honored grads, fifteen years after they have finally made it through high school.)

_____ and her husband, _____, are celebrating their tin wedding anniversary, twelve years of eating out of cans.
_____ had a hard time deciding on a career. At first, she planned to be a violinist, but discovered she was too high

146

strung. Then she tried professional bowling, but that wasn't up her alley. Next, she had a compulsion to be a magician, but the urge suddenly vanished. She also studied to be a librarian, but she finally shelved that idea. She also thought about being a plumber, but that was just a pipe dream. Eventually, though, our _____ made her mark in the world. She will go down in history with the new diet she invented. It's called the Chinese Diet. You get all you want to eat, but you only get to use one chopstick.

*   *   *

Then there's _____. Now there's a success! In fact, _____ was so successful at so many things that he decided to combine his multiple talents into a many-faceted career. As this generation's answer to the Mickey Mouse Club, _____ has his own TV series, on which he plays a comic MD. He's also gone into the recording field and has several new albums out. Some of his hit discs are: "The Object of My Injection," "Liver, Come Back to Me," "Has Anybody Seen My Gall?" and "Tie a Yellow Ribbon 'round the Old Appendectomy." Off stage, _____ is a real doctor, and for awhile his specialty was curing windbags with acupuncture. But now he's really gotten smart. He gave up acupuncture when he realized it was more profitable to stick patients with his bill.

*   *   *

_____, bless his pea-picking heart, bombed out as a band director. _____ started out teaching music in elementary schools, where he soon learned that little kids don't bring apples to the teacher anymore—instead, they drive 'em bananas. He then tried the entertainment field, billed as "Satchmo _____." He was a great success until he blew too hard. You guessed it! He blew his brains out. Now he's

147

teaching history at a junior college, because everybody knows you don't need any brains to be a history teacher. Here's a sample of what he's teaching: "Shakespeare married an Avon lady"; "Paul Revere was an alarmist"; "The Wright Brothers were just plane folks"; and "Whistler's mother was framed."

*   *   *

Using a Charlie Brown joke book, select appropriate gags for the various members of your group and include them in the program. During the evening, have the teens read their own lines. They could be listed like this:

Overheard by the Great Pumpkin

Reader One: "But you don't understand! I'm like Samson. Take away this long hair, man, and I'm nothing!"

Reader Two: "What do you mean I'm not ambitious? I'm trying to be the world's greatest teenager! How ambitious can you get?"

Reader Three: "I have three jazz albums, two symphony albums, and sixty-eight religious albums. If that isn't real spirituality, I don't know what is!"

Reader Four: "I take my religious beliefs seriously. I get into arguments almost every day!"

Reader Five: "I had to give up having a secret closet of prayer. Every time I went in there, all those cashmere sweaters made me feel guilty!"

*   *   *

The reading of the class's last will and testament is always a fun time. Again, write a goofy will for each of your grads and try to include the names of as many underclassmen as you can. Some idea starters:

Good Grief, Charlie Brown!

We, the class of _____, residents of Goof-off Corner, locally known as the left rear pews of (name of church), being of some (?) mind and sound body (youth's name), or sound mind and some (!) body (youth's name), do hereby declare this to be our last will and testament:

I, _____, bequeath my shy manner and winsome ways to (underclassman). My masculine charm, which has won me a flock of female admirers, goes to _____—he can also have the admirers. My Charles Atlas Body Building course I donate to _____ with the sincere hope that it does him more good than it did me. I have a new and unused razor, which I humbly present to _____. And last, but far from least, my size 13 sneakers I graciously pass on to _____; he's the only one around who can fill my shoes!

I, _____, bequeath my superb trumpet playing ability, especially on offertories, to _____. My position as Big Boss and Bully of the _____ Clan goes to my sister and heir apparent, _____. My dearest and richest treasure, my Nash heap, I will to the nearest junk yard. _____ can have my broad shoulders and rippling biceps, and _____ is the recipient of my love for flying. And I gladly give my ten o'clock curfew to _____ and _____.

I, _____, do will and bequeath my sweet spirit and quiet ways to _____. _____ can have my willingness to sing solos, and I understand that _____ would dearly love to have my ability to get prom dates, especially with _____. My fantastic acting ability I pass on to _____; and my treasurer's job to anyone who can add.

*   *   *

No Peanuts program could be complete without *Lucy's Advice Column*. Fill this page with humorous Lucy-type

149

advice. For example, Lucy would no doubt offer gems like these:

- "As you slide down the bannister of life, make sure the splinters never point your way."

- "A gentleman is a man who holds the door open while his wife carries in the groceries."

- "Make certain you always have a verse of scripture to back up one of your preconceived notions."

Devotions

Since a special speaker is usually featured at this type of gathering, no other devotions are needed. However, the speaker should be informed of the theme, so the message can be tied in with it. The speaker may want to joke about Charlie Brown's loser image, then emphasize how to be a winner for God. Or the speaker may pick up on the "What Next?" idea and zero in on some segment of the future, college or careers.

Madrigal Dinner

BANQUETING MADRIGAL STYLE

Back in the Middle Ages, the serfs toiled away as the landed gentry celebrated in a style never again to be matched for its pomp and circumstance, combined with a good measure of merriment.

Revive the Middle Ages by turning an annual church banquet into the fête of the century. Do you have a church bowling team or league? Present the trophies and accolades with a Cavalier Bowlers Banquet. Or announce the "Ye Olde Victorie Banquete" to celebrate a church team's impressive record in softball or basketball. If you want to celebrate Christmas in a traditional way, this is the banquet for you.

Decorations

Turn the room into a medieval banquet hall or early American country inn. To create the medieval mood, set candles in heavy metal candlesticks for centerpieces. Arrange fencing foils, swords, shields, and football or motorcycle helmets covered in foil around the room. Drape a chair in royal colors for a throne for the master of ceremonies. Place standards and family crests artfully around the room.

If early America is your era, use hurricane lamps on the tables, with wooden trays and heavy plates and pottery to enhance the atmosphere. Have people bring in their braided rugs, embroidered samplers, and quilted wall hangings for further decor.

Ask the participants to dress the part of landed gentry. Knickers can easily be made by tucking trouser legs into knee-high socks. If you're going medieval, dress someone as the court jester.

Menu

Roast beef, baked potatoes, figgy pudding, trifle, and hot cider will tempt the palate and fill the bill for even the most royal lord and lady.

Program

Programs should be printed using archaic English spellings and words. A program used for a bowling banquet opened this way:

"Tonight as we lift our glasses in a toast to another successful Cavalier bowling season, we greet all our friends . . .

"Welcome, Lords and Ladies, to the Great Hall of the landed gentry, where we will enjoy an evening of spontaneous hilarity and merrymaking."

After welcoming the guests, the host of the evening reads the Rules of Etyquette or Common Curtasye:

I. Guestes must have nailes cleane or they wille disgust their table companiones.
II. Guestes must avoid quarrelinge and making grimaces with other guestes.
III. Guestes must not stuff their mouths.
IV. Guestes sholde not pick their teethe with a knife, strawe, or sticke.
V. Guestes must never leave bones on the table; always hide them under the chaires.
VI. Guestes must not tell unseemely tales at the table, nor soile the clothe with their knives, nor rest their legges upon the table.

VII. Guestes must not wipe their greasy fingers on their beardes.

VIII. Guestes must not leane on the table with their elbowes, nor dip their thumbs into their drinkes.

IX. Guestes must retaine their knives or they shal be forced to grubbe with their fingers.

X. Guestes who must burpe must do so quietly and discreetely.

The host then gives the invocation, which is followed by Victuals, Viands, and Vin. Here the guests are encouraged to "eat heartily, happily, and heavily"—at least until the food runs out!

The program concludes with Revelrie and Merrymakinge. "All guestes will please participate to the best of their abilitie."

During the Revelrie and Merrymakinge, have a group of minstrels or a brass ensemble entertain with songs reminiscent of the era. At Christmas, sing the traditional Christmas carols, such as "Silent Night" and "O, Little Town of Bethlehem." Have your jester(s) prance around the room doing mischief and mayhem. If you have a resident juggler, sword swallower, or contortionist, put that person on center stage.

If you are celebrating a sports event, present your trophies and laurels. It's great fun to have someone put together a videotape of the sports season's more hilarious moments for a surprising showing at the banquet.

Devotions

If you're using this for Christmas, retell the story of the writing of a Christmas carol. For a sports event, use scriptures such as Hebrews 12:1-2 or I Corinthians 9:24-27.

Simple
Suggestions

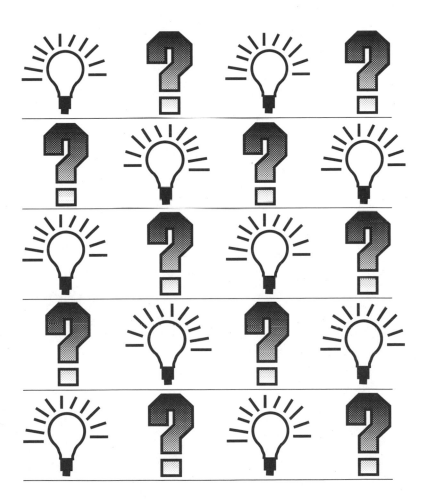

Last-Minute Creations

IDEAS AND SUGGESTIONS

Sunday service has come to an end. You're standing around greeting your friends. Someone taps you on the shoulder and, with a dazzling smile, says, "We're having a potluck next Sunday. I was supposed to be in charge of it, but I have to be out of town next week. Would you be a dear and . . ."

Before you hit the aspirin bottle or resort to pulling out your hair, take heart. You can have a creative potluck without a month's worth of elaborate planning.

Give your potluck a new direction by going backward. Serve the food in reverse order, with the desserts first and the salads last. For added fun, have everyone dress backward, or inside-out.

Deck the tables with inside-out tablecloths and upside-down centerpieces. If the place settings are on the table, turn the plates upside down and the utensils in reverse order and upside down—fork on the right side with knife and spoon on the left. Dishes such as pineapple upside down cake and tossed salads go well with a topsy-turvy meal.

For an even simpler meal, for which no program is planned, there are a myriad of possibilities for getting away from the usual potluck fare. Have chili 101 different ways, with everyone

157

bringing his or her favorite chili recipe. Or announce "Soup's on" and have each family bring a special soup.

Other meal ideas include a Crockpot Supper, to which everyone brings something prepared in a slow cooker. This is great for a warm meal after a wintertime outing. Just make sure you have enough outlets to keep all the cookers going.

How about a salad or pita sandwich bar? Provide the lettuce while everyone else brings something to pile on—olives, tomatoes, cheese, sliced eggs, onions, avocados, fruits, meats, and so on.

Or for the sandwich bar, have each family bring enough pita rounds for every family member, plus a meat or relish for the sandwiches. Serve both meals salad bar style.

To make your potluck ethnic, try a "Bagel Bash." All this requires is plenty of bagels and enough chutzpah to experiment. If you're not bound by the kosher laws, don't be afraid to try cheeses and various meats on the bagels.

While cream cheese and lox are the traditional accompaniment to a bagel, you can also pair them with salmon spread, cheese spreads, or cream cheese and jam. Bagels also make a great foundation for miniature pizzas, cinnamon toast, or meats and gravy.

The same type of imagination and creativity can build a supper on a Mexican tortilla, which can be heated on an open fire, grilled, deep fried, or baked crisp.

Other quick meal ideas include "Potluck Pie," "Strictly Fingers," or "Try for a Record."

For "Potluck Pie," everyone brings some kind of pie—tamale pie, pizza pie, shepherd's pie, hamburger pie, and, of course, all of the traditional dessert pies. A good cookbook index can give you enough pie ideas for several potlucks.

"Strictly Fingers" means finger food only. This works well for a quick get-together following an evening service, a singspiration, or a film. Since all food must be eaten with the fingers, you save on a lot of cleanup time, as there will be no dirty

utensils to collect and wash. Beware, though; invariably someone brings something that requires a fork. If this happens, smile
and break out the silverware.

"Try for the Record" can be lots of fun as the group bands
together to create the world's largest hoagie, biggest banana
split, or tallest stack of pancakes. Folks of all ages enjoy the
hilarity, but this idea works especially well for youth group
gatherings.

Menu ideas aren't the only things that can pep up your
potluck. Sometimes a move as simple as taking the food
outdoors can do wonders for the atmosphere. If your church
doesn't have a nice lawn for a picnic, use the parking lot or
migrate to a nearby park.

Having everyone dress for the occasion does a great deal to set
a mood, too. Follow the lead of the grocery store chains when
they go all out for Hawaiian or Western days and have their help
all decked out in appropriate attire. This is a good way to set a
light mood for what can turn into a long-remembered time of
fun and fellowship.

While most people enjoy masquerading in outlandish costumes, they also enjoy a chance to dress in their finest. In
today's casual society, there are few chances to dress formally
outside of high school and college functions. Give your group
an excuse to dig out those fancy clothes that hang forever in the
back of the closet.

A church potluck props box, or cabinet or shelf, contains
photos, calendar pictures, flowers, and all the makings for a
variety of centerpieces. Anything that could add to potluck
decor goes into this box, making your scrounging that much
easier.

Some great things for the prop box are an assortment of
stickers and freebies. The stickers can help build a theme when
placed on plastic utensils, cups, plates, and tablecloths.

Freebies include the recipes for punch and easy meals that
are available from food manufacturers and many grocers. Your

grocer may also have free brochures on party ideas. Other freebies are available in the form of promotional materials from specific food industries, such as the Idaho Potato Commission or the American Dairy Association. Many travel agencies and theaters will give away old promotional posters that can be used to spiff up your potluck's decor.

Haunt garage sales and thrift shops for other great potluck bargains. Old vases, costume jewelry, silk flowers, seashells, and other goodies can be picked up for a song and added to your potluck props box.

Something as simple as a change in table coverings can add a great deal to your potluck. Rolls of blank newsprint are available at most newspaper offices, some for free and some for mere pennies per pound. They are a perfect size for most banquet tables and lend themselves to crayons, water colors, and markers if you want to exercise your artistic flare. Newsprint is much cheaper and more durable than standard white tablecloth rolls.

Plain white flat sheets also work well. Use double bed size for a nice draped effect; twin size gives a more casual look. Scrounge the remnant tables at fabric shops for colorful table coverings. Widths from 54- to 60-inches usually need only a quick hem at each end to become acceptable tablecloths. Bedspreads, quilts, and printed flat sheets also work as creative table backgrounds.

In planning your potluck, remember to include everyone in the church. Having everyone help will give people a unique chance to use their God-given talents, to share a cherished collection, and to feel a part of the "inner circle" of doers. You may also discover a wealth of talent you didn't know existed!

Beverages for a Crowd

PUNCH

Beverage recipes are a dime a dozen, yet many groups still run to the supermarket and buy canned varieties. When you've spent hours on planning, decorations, and a great menu, don't spoil the party with a boring drink! Try some of these recipes for an added "kick."

Frozen Fruit Slush

1 cup sugar
1 lb. frozen strawberries
3 mashed bananas
1 each 6 ox. can frozen orange juice and lemon juice (diluted as directed)
1 small jar maraschino cherries and juice
1 medium can chunk pineapple and juice

Mix and freeze. Set out 2 hours ahead of time to let thaw. Serve in punch bowl with orange and lemon slices.

Garbage Can Punch

1 lb. package lemonade mix
1 large can frozen orange juice
1 large can frozen grape or cherry juice
1 qt. 7-Up
1 can mandarin orange slices
1 small jar maraschino cherries

Dilute and mix lemonade and frozen juices as directed. Just before serving, add 7-Up, orange slices, and cherries.

Cheap and Easy Punch

2 small packages Kool-Aid, any flavor
1 can frozen fruit juice
Sugar to taste
Large bottle of chilled ginger ale, 7-Up, Squirt, or Sprite

Mix Kool-Aid with three qts. cold water. Add diluted juice, sugar, and pop. Pour over ice cubes. For a frothy drink, use complementary-flavored sherbet in a punch bowl.

Tip: For an elegant color-matched punch, simply pour a clear soda over whatever flavor sherbet matches your color scheme. Great for wedding receptions!

Gelatin Punch

Make 3 boxes gelatin (cherry or raspberry). Dissolve 2-3 cups sugar in hot gelatin. Add 2 cans each frozen lemonade and frozen orange juice, diluted as directed, 1 large can pineapple juice, and 1½ large bottles of ginger ale.

Cinnamon Christmas Punch

Pre-chill eight 3 liter bottles of cola. Then pour ice-cold cola into punch bowl. Add one tray of orange-cinnamon ice cubes. (To make cubes, heat ¼ cup cinnamon candies with ½ cup water, stirring until candies are dissolved. Add 3 cups orange juice, pour into ice cube tray and freeze.) Float orange slices in punch. Makes twelve 8 oz. servings.

Hot Chocolate Mix

To make 150 cups of hot chocolate, mix together one 8 qt. box instant milk, 1 lb. box Nestles' Quick, a 3 oz. jar of Coffee Mate, and 1 lb. box powdered sugar. Use about ⅓ cup mix to 1 cup hot water.

Hot Punch

4 tea bags
4 sticks cinnamon
6 whole cloves
2 qts. boiling water
½ cup sugar
1 cup lemon juice
1 cup orange juice
1 qt. pineapple juice
2 cups cranberry juice cocktail
2 qts. apple cider
2 qts. ginger ale

Put tea bags, cinnamon, and cloves in boiling water; steep 10 minutes. Remove. Add sugar, juices, and cider. Heat to boiling, stirring frequently. Pour ginger ale into 2 gallon container; then pour in hot tea mixture. (If using a glass punch bowl, place a metal spoon in the bowl to prevent hot liquid from breaking the glass.)

Quantities

GUESS HOW MANY ARE COMING TO DINNER?

Figuring quantities for large crowds of people can be a real mind-boggler. The following chart should make your food committee's job a bit easier.

Quantity Per 100 People

Coffee—3 lbs.
Sugar—3 lbs.
Cream—3 qts.
Whipping Cream—4 pts.
Milk—6 gal.
Fruit Cocktail—2½ gal.
Fruit or Tomato Juice—four no. 10 cans
Oysters—18 qts.
Hot Dogs—25 lbs.
Meat Loaf—24 lbs.
Ham, Roast Beef, or Roast Pork—40 lbs.
Hamburger—30-36 lbs.
Chicken—40 lbs.
Potatoes—35 lbs.
Scalloped Potatoes—5 gal.
Vegetables—four no. 10 cans

Baked Beans—5 gal.
Cauliflower—18 lbs.
Cabbage for Coleslaw—20 lbs.
Carrots—33 lbs.
Bread—10 loaves
Rolls—200
Butter or margarine—3 lbs.
Potato Salad—12 qts.
Fruit Salad—20 qts.
Vegetable Salad—20 qts.
Lettuce—20 heads
Salad Dressing—3 qts.
Pies—18
Cakes—8, 9 x 13, bundt, or two layer
Ice Cream—4 gal.
Cheese—3 lbs.
Olives or Pickles—2 qts.
Nuts—3 lbs.

Be Creative!

LET THE BEAUTY OF JESUS BE SEEN
IN YOUR EFFORTS

The first thing we learn about Jesus in the Gospel of John is that he was active in the creation of the world. John 1:1-3 declares that without Jesus nothing was made that has been made. Think about it! Our Savior, Jesus Christ, is also our Creator. The innovator, the artist, the designer of beauty—our God, who made all things bright and beautiful!

Imagine being there at the dawn of creation, when the morning stars sang together, when the mists rose from the towering mountains, when the graceful horses stretched their slender legs for the first time, when the water first began its bubbling, tumbling course through the woods, over the rocks, down the hillside.

Envision some of the beauty and infinite variety our God created—sparkling waterfalls, serene lakes, giant redwoods, gentle breezes, fields of perfect flowers. And God continues to create. We have a different sunset every night. In the winter, there are fluffy snowflakes, each one an original design. And think of little children, each a squirming, wriggling mass of human potential.

Even in our personal lives, God takes all the mistakes, all the broken pieces, and all the false starts and weaves them into the tapestry of our lives, creating something beautiful.

Since the Bible tells us that we are created in the image of God, doesn't it follow that some of God's majestic creativity will show through in our lives? If we really want God's beauty to be seen in us, where, then, is there any place in our lives for a blah, bland Christianity? Those of us who claim to walk with God should certainly be the most creative.

Creative Christians have no place in their churches for ho-hum, slap-dash dinners. "But," you protest, "I'm just not a creative person! I could never . . . "

Our smallness comes from our desire to play it safe. We look at our own abilities, or lack of them, our own enthusiasm, or lack of it. Our scared littleness keeps us in a box. Creativity demands risks.

Using our creativity stretches us, makes us reach out to others, finds us doing things we never thought we could do. What if you can't carry a tune in a bushel basket or draw anything but flies? What if your church is tiny, financially embarrassed, lacking in talent, or all of the above?

Don't sing, don't design a masterpiece, don't plan a formal sit-down dinner for five hundred people. Find something your own size. In other words, express yourself. As Shakespeare said, "to thine own self be true."

Smallness or lack of funds are simply minor obstacles on the road to great church fellowships. Use them as challenges to your creativity. Who knows? Maybe a few fun-filled dinners will help your church outgrow that smallness and lack of funds!

Indexes

General Index

ADDRESSES

American Bible Society, 49
American Board of Missions to the
Jews, 20
Bible Pathways, 49
Bible Visuals, Inc., 116
Idaho Potato Commission, 22
Moody Films, 130
Rio Grande Bible College, 130
The Evangelical Alliance Mission, 93

GAMES

Charades, 19
Cork or ping-pong ball harvest, 43
Crab-leg relay, 43
Frog-jumping contest, 122
Horse, 16
Lifesaver-on-a-toothpick relay,
109
Mummy wrap, 108
Mystery auction, 108
Obstacle course, 115
Sadie Hawkins' Day race, 119
Scavenger hunt variations, 119
Shipwreck, 43
Snowball relay, 16
Snowball 21, 16
Stool ball, 115
Water balloon toss, 43

Water feed, 108
Watermelon scramble, 43

LYRICS

"Cristo Me Ama," 36
"Hey Diddle Diddle," 136
"Onward Christian Parents," 29
"Until They Know," 93
"We've a Song to Sing About Parents," 29

OCCASIONS

Anglers' breakfast, 91
Anniversary celebration, 28
Annual banquet, 151
Appreciation dinner, 81, 105
Armed Forces Day, 26, 101
Athletic banquet, 46, 101, 151
Baby shower, 87, 124
Birthday party, 41
Black history month, 18
Bridal shower, 87
Camp, 76
Canadian Thanksgiving, 48
Careers Day, 99
Children's parties, 124
Choir parties, 110
Christian school awards banquet, 49
Christmas, 53, 153
Christmas in July, 40

171

RECIPES

Scripture Index